HOW TO GET THE BEST OUT OF YOUR LAWYER

Disclaimer

While every care has been taken in the production of this book, no legal responsibility is accepted, warranted or implied by the author, editor or publisher in respect of any errors, omissions or mis-statements. You should always seek professional or legal advice from a suitably qualified person when appropriate.

HOW TO GET THE BEST OUT OF YOUR LAWYER

A Guide to Engaging the Services of Legal Professionals

Bart D. Daly

ORPEN PRESS

Published by
Orpen Press
Lonsdale House
Avoca Avenue
Blackrock
Co. Dublin
Ireland

e-mail: info@orpenpress.com
www.orpenpress.com

Paperback ISBN 978-1-871305-78-4
ePub ISBN 978-1-871305-90-6
Kindle ISBN 978-1-871305-91-3

Printed and bound by CPI Group (UK) Ltd, Croydon, CR0 4YY

To Stephanie, Harrison, Hannah-Sioux and Poppy

Foreword

For the majority of consumers the engagement of and with legal professionals is an uncomfortable one. This is because there are so many varied and personally challenging elements involved that must be comprehensively addressed and dealt with. Generally, and certainly until the publication of this guide, that engagement has involved little, if any, knowledge or understanding of the protocols that should be determined by the consumer for the service from the outset and throughout the arrangement.

What is special about this much appreciated and long-needed guide is that Bart Daly provides Irish consumers with specialist information and education in clear and readily understandable terms – something of a rarity in the area of legal tomes. Here he provides what will be for a great many readers an illuminating and positive step-by-step pathway that permits full insight into and a clear understanding of our varied legal services and their providers. He achieves this by setting out those steps that must, of necessity, be taken by both customer and advisor if they are to jointly, affordably and successfully engage.

Importantly too, this is a guide for both the personal and the business consumer of these essential inescapable life-demanding service engagements. For many, the choice of solicitor or legal advisor comes through the recommendation of family or friends. Word of mouth plays a large part here. Now though, at long last, we have here the means to exercise personal consumer choice from an informed position. This is because the practicalities are addressed comprehensively in the guide. The dos and don'ts are well-signalled and allow the consumer prepare and outline, specifically, what are their needs and expectations. We learn of the importance of communicating, of questioning, of comprehensively conferring and of keeping records, notes and copies of all documentation. Of primary importance, always, is cost and Bart does not glance across the issue in general terms but rather he focuses clearly on the need to know, at all times, what are the costs and why they are necessitated. He balances his advice by reminding the reader that we are dealing with experts here whose expertise has a value that must also be acknowledged and regarded. *Quid pro quo* takes its rightful place alongside *caveat emptor*.

The provision and protection of our rights, the entitlement to our due respect and the protection of what is ours – whether it be our land, our family, our good name, our personal information or our last wishes for those we hold near and dear – all require the oversight and professional consideration of lawyers. Bart ensures that he equips us with the means of determining our needs, of preparing our questions and of communicating them with confidence. With this guide comes a rare opportunity to take control of your requirements and in so doing dispense with that worry that has until now left you uncomfortable and therefore at a distinct disadvantage at these most important of occasions and interactions with members of the legal profession.

It is a pleasure to introduce a book that presents the opportunity to benefit so many consumers on what will be the many different occasions occurring throughout the course of their lives and the lives of their families. This gem provides a clear, concise and understandable explanation for the consumer that empowers them to personally facilitate a resolution of their legal problems and requirements.

Bart Daly has written this guide for you. It is your need that is prioritised here and you will not be disappointed.

Dermott Jewell
Chief Executive
Consumers' Association of Ireland
31 August 2012

Preface

It is inevitable that at some stage you will need a lawyer. Like every profession or trade, there are good ones and not so good ones. However, ending up with the latter may simply be a matter of choosing the wrong one. But it should not be a case of good luck in finding the best lawyer for you.

This book is intended to help you make an informed choice and get the best lawyer for your particular need.

I use the general term 'lawyer' as it is commonly used, even though in Ireland it is technically incorrect. Here we use solicitors and barristers and I distinguish them in their roles within the book. When referring to both of them I use the word 'lawyer'. A solicitor is your first port of call; they advise clients on legal matters, represent clients in certain lower courts, and prepare cases for barristers to present in the higher courts. A barrister is brought in by a solicitor for cases that go before the higher courts. The thrust of this book will deal with solicitors.

Lawyers are commonly brought in after a problem has arisen and often the client has an expectation that the lawyer will 'sort it'.

Lawyers are trained and experienced at advising on a variety of legal matters and initiating or defending litigation. They are not magicians, so the client should have realistic expectations of the outcome once the lawyer is on board.

The intervention of a lawyer can bring about a positive outcome or reduce the exposure you might otherwise have, but these are dependent on a whole range of factors. For this reason a (good) lawyer will not make statements like 'we will win this case'. They can offer their opinion on whether your case is strong or weak, subject to a complete appraisal of the facts.

I hope readers will find this book a useful guide to engaging the services of legal professionals. They are there to help you and if you have a clear understanding of how the system works this should remove any of the unknown factors and enable you work with your lawyer for a common purpose and result.

I would like to thank Dermott Jewell, Chief Executive of the Consumers' Association of Ireland, for reading this book and writing the foreword. As the book is intended for consumers and corporate markets, his involvement is most appropriate and indeed welcome.

I would also like to acknowledge and thank the Courts Service of Ireland for permission to reproduce Appendix I: The Courts and the Law Society of Ireland for permission to reproduce Appendix III: Periods of Limitation. The Bar Council of

Ireland kindly read over the section applicable to barristers – my thanks goes to them too.

The Legal Aid Board and Free Legal Advice Centres (FLAC) were very helpful in providing details of the law centres and legal advice centres they run throughout the country, details of which are included in the Useful Addresses section at the back of this book.

Additionally, Ian Toomey of Ian Toomey and Associates provided very helpful feedback on the views of the SME sector.

I would like to thank Brian Walker, BL for casting his eye over the chapter on alternative dispute resolution and offering helpful comments.

I would also like to thank those other individuals and legal professionals who read through the book and provided feedback. Such assistance proved invaluable.

My use of English was improved by Hannah-Sioux Daly before submission to the publisher. With regard to the latter I would like to thank Gerry O'Connor of Orpen Press and, in particular, I would like to thank my editor, Eileen O'Brien, who was most patient with me and thoroughly professional in her work.

The opinions expressed in this book are entirely my own.

Bart D. Daly
Dublin
2 September 2012

Contents

Contents

1

Choosing a Solicitor

In many ways this is the most important chapter
in this book.

You have a problem. To you, it's important and
you need to get it resolved. You may have tried
to resolve it yourself but failed and (unknow-
ingly) possibly made things worse. Many people
or proprietors of small businesses try to sort out
disputes themselves or draft what they believe is
a straight-forward contract without legal advice.
In some cases that is fine, but where they find
themselves unable to do so and they then bring
in a lawyer, it may be too late to resolve the
problem and so the lawyer's job is one of damage
limitation.

A good example of the above can be seen in
cases coming before the Employment Appeals
Tribunal. By the time the solicitor comes on board
the damage is often done. Here the law is written
with the employee in mind. Even with the best

of intentions, good employers can find they have transgressed the law by some procedure or lack of procedure.

When two parties are contracting they may submit to paper what their respective roles are. At this time there is goodwill between the parties and eagerness to get on with the business. In some such situations they may commit to paper the 'arrangement' between them. They may be friends or even related and may not feel the need for a formal contract. *This is a recipe for disaster.* People fall out. Then one of the parties goes to their solicitor, and guess what? One could drive tractors through the gaps in the contract. These situations can be very hard to solve and costly too.

So you have a problem and it needs sorting. You may have used a solicitor in the past. Don't automatically lift the phone to ring 'your' solicitor. Ask yourself, 'Is this solicitor right for this problem?'

You may know solicitors from a sporting club or socially and they are nice people. Sure they are, but do they have the right experience to take your problem on?

A solicitor's work may be associated with solving legal problems, but their skill also is in preventing legal problems. The wisdom of engaging a solicitor to advise you on dealing with consumer or commercial issues surrounding the introduction of a new product or service could save your company thousands of Euro if any claims arise and you have in place, thanks to the solicitor, the means to deal with it without the loss of valuable man-hours and money.

So how do you choose the right solicitor?

Horses for Courses

If you have a sore back and you know of a GP who has a good reputation for bad backs do you go to them or to your own GP and hope for the best? Well, the same applies to solicitors. Most law firms have a general practice and their websites will tell you the areas of law they practise in. So if you have a copyright problem and your usual solicitor's firm doesn't list intellectual property on its website, or it does but with little emphasis, then that firm is not for you.

If you have a good relationship with a solicitor you have used in the past but believe that solicitor may not have the experience in your particular area of concern you could contact them and ask them to refer you to a solicitor with the expertise you need. This may be a good starting point but nonetheless, before following up on the name, you should still conduct your own research. Also, if you do use the referred solicitor enquire from them when discussing fees whether you are paying a referral fee too.

Before you ask around, do your own research. Google solicitors in Ireland with the area of law your problem is in. Ask people you know if they can recommend anyone.

You can decide whether you want a big, medium or small firm. The size of firm does not necessarily mean it is better. The bigger ones will be more expensive and they will have highly skilled solicitors employed. But there are many smaller firms with particular expertise and lower cost that are just as good.

When choosing a solicitor it is wise to find one who has experience in the area of law of interest to you. So if you want a specialist – that is a solicitor with a lot of experience in the area you require – then eliminate the firms that appear to have a general practice.

When you think you have found a solicitor or drawn up a shortlist, ask around if people you know have used them and what they thought of them.

While law firms' websites are informative, they are not objective so you need to do your homework. The more time you put into finding the solicitor for you the better chance of getting one suited to your business or problem, so you start with a feeling of confidence in your choice of lawyer.

Fees

Ask around for what people paid for solicitors. This will give you a general 'feel' for this important matter. Look to see if their websites cover fees. Not many do but where this is the case this is useful information for you before initiating contact.

The fees question is very important so do as much research as you can on this matter before meeting the solicitor. At this stage you are only getting ballpark figures but it prepares you for the outlay you will incur and it's better to have a real understanding of this before venturing further.

There is a difference between advisory work and litigation. In the former the expertise is within the law firm so here you are paying the hourly rate and fees should be easier to estimate. In litigation, solicitors acting for you will incur costs in issuing the proceedings so it is not unreasonable for solicitors to seek some costs upfront for this. Also in litigation, surprises can occur adding time to the preparation of the case and making it harder to pin down the cost.

Do all this before you make contact with the solicitor.

Litigation Considerations

If the matter you are seeking advice on is contentious and litigation is likely then remember the solicitor spends most of their time in their office and not in the courtroom. Certainly the solicitor will research the matter, and consult the legislation and case law before forming an opinion on where your case is going. Where the solicitor advises bringing counsel (i.e. a barrister) in, they will, when advising counsel, often venture their take on the case.

Preferably sound out this from the solicitor at the first meeting. If the solicitor believes the case will be a 'fighter', have they dealt with similar cases in the past? If so, how do they see your case panning out? The solicitor can only express their opinion as every case is different and contains different elements, and while the case may be in the same area of law, there are so many permutations that the solicitor will not be able to predict the outcome but only offer their opinion based on their experience.

It is at this stage that the possibility of settlement can be discussed and when would be the best time to raise this with the other side. Whether your solicitor makes the first move or awaits an approach from the other side is a matter for them (see Chapters 9 and 10). Negotiation is a skill and needs to be dealt with in a strategic way. Before that is considered, your case's strengths and weaknesses have to be assessed.

Clients' 'Do' List

- Do conduct research on finding a solicitor for you
- Do seek a solicitor who has experience in the area you need

Clients' 'Don't' List

- Don't try to solve a legal issue yourself; seek help
- Don't rush in engaging a solicitor; make your choice after careful research

2

What Services Do Solicitors Provide?

People often associate solicitors with litigation and indeed sometimes people's first contact with solicitors is when they are being sued or want to sue. But the converse is the reality of solicitors' work.

The range of solicitors' work is considerable and mostly non-contentious, such as conveyancing, wills, divorce, contracts and advisory work.

Those engaged in commercial life would benefit from solicitors' advice on:

- Setting up a new business
- Employee rights and employee contracts
- Sale and acquisition of assets
- Commercial contracts
- Environmental issues
- Health and safety issues
- Fraud
- Employee termination

- Data protection
- Product liability
- Professional liability
- Information technology issues
- Tribunal representation

Many of the above can create legal issues which, if not handled properly, have the potential to incur financial loss, whereas preventive legal advice can avert trouble and save money. The corporate sector has a considerable body of regulatory obligations to comply with so getting legal advice to prevent future problems arising make sense.

Individuals too can avail of solicitors' advice on a whole range of issues, such as:

- Disputes with neighbours
- Wills
- Divorce, marital problems and children
- Sale or purchase of a house or land
- Adoption
- Consumer rights
- Immigration
- Defamation
- Criminal law

Most law firms will handle criminal law as part of their general practice; however there are specialist criminal law firms too and for serious criminal law offences these should be strongly considered for their specialist expertise.

Solicitors, and indeed barristers, also work in tribunals such as the Employment Appeals Tribunal, Equality Tribunal and Labour Court.

3

First Contact with the Solicitor

Okay, so now you have done your due diligence and are about to contact the selected solicitor.

It is critically important that for this meeting you either take notes yourself or bring a good note-taker. These notes may be referred to a lot later on, particularly if the relationship with your solicitor sours.

Before the meeting, open a file to record all correspondence that will be exchanged once the solicitor has been engaged. Retain a copy of all documentation you hand over to the solicitor. If they are original documents indicate them as such. There may be witnesses you need; contact them and ascertain if they are willing to give evidence. Gather names, addresses, mobile numbers, email addresses, dates, incidents, etc.

Make a checklist of all the issues you need to discuss with the solicitor. At the conclusion of the meeting, check the list to ensure you have covered all the points.

The first meeting is exploratory. You are there to ascertain for yourself that this solicitor is who you want. You will be weighing them up and they too will be weighing you up. First impressions are very important. Most first meetings or consultations are free but be sure to check this at the time of first contact. Don't be afraid to enquire if the solicitor has had cases similar to yours in the past and how much experience they have in the relevant area.

Solicitors are human like the rest of us and come in diverse personalities. While as a group they tend to be conservative, some would be more conservative than others. This you will see from the initial meeting and you need to decide whether you think you can work with this person. Will they be running your case or another solicitor in the firm? If the latter, you need to meet that person. Will your personalities work or clash?

Things to Watch Out For

Attentiveness

Is the solicitor a good listener, are they taking notes, are they punctual, have they devoted uninterrupted time to this consultation and not allowed the consultation be disturbed with phone calls, texts and emails? An exception to this would be a litigation solicitor, where their time often over-runs with cases running late and so on, but this should be explained from the outset.

A Presumption that You Are Already a Client

If this is the case you need to put the brakes on and remind them that this is an exploratory meeting.

Vagueness on Questions Asked

Not getting clear answers is a worrying signal. You must emerge from the meeting with a clear understanding of the issues raised.

An Over-Enthusiastic Lawyer

Most solicitors are conservative so if you come across an over-eager one, beware.

If you ask the solicitor at the exploratory meeting what are your chances of success having outlined the case, most solicitors will be careful in their response; so if you come across one who gives you the feeling it is an open and shut case it's time to move on to the next name on your list. There are too many unknown factors in litigation to consider before predicting success. There is nothing wrong in saying you appear to have a good or strong case but so early in the process anything more is reck-less and misleading.

Fees

Fees can be a thorny issue so it is best to tackle it early to avoid any misunderstandings later. It would be good to state at the start that your budget is limited so you need to know exactly what the costs will be and how they are structured. Many solicitors charge by the hour. Partners will charge more than assistant solicitors. You need to know who is handling your case (it is not necessarily the person you meet at the introductory meeting). On being told the hourly rates you need to ask if one solicitor or more be involved. If you get an answer like 'it is not envisaged more than one will be required' you need to get clarification on this as that answer leaves the door open to another solicitor joining the team and your fees escalating. It is reasonable to enquire into the role of apprentices and if you are paying for them.

If the solicitor says they can only estimate the fees this would be a concern and needs further probing. You need to know the fee exposure you will be incurring.

Normally, upfront advances of fees should be avoided but in the current climate it may not be unreasonable if the sum sought is reasonable and in the form of a deposit.

Don't get too hung up on comparing hourly rates among law firms; a highly experienced specialist may charge a higher rate but they are more likely to get the work done more quickly. The key point here is to get an estimate of how many hours the job will take.

If the notes taken at the explanatory meeting estimate the work is to be done in, say, fifty fee-paying hours and you get a bill for considerably in excess of that you will have the notes of your exploratory meeting to dispute the increased fee. The solicitor will have to justify the significant increase in fee. With what had been agreed at the initial meeting, unless the solicitor can show they alerted you to the increase in fees, they will have a difficult job in justifying the increase and even less chance of getting it.

When the solicitor has been engaged it can be useful to agree a staged payment of their fee. This is good for the solicitor but better for you as you will avoid a big bill at the conclusion of the work and will be able to stay on budget as the work progresses.

In litigation you need to be aware that if you lose you will be paying your costs and the other party's costs. Weigh this up before taking a case.

In addition to fees, solicitors often charge for 'outlay' such as couriers, phone calls, photocopy-ing and stamps so at this meeting ask about these items too. Some firms may cover these costs in their overhead but it is another cost you need to know about.

At the conclusion of your exploratory meeting you have to feel confident that this solicitor will be competent to handle your work. You also need to be completely satisfied with the fee structure. (See Chapter 6 for more on fees.)

Statutory Obligations of Solicitors

Solicitors are compelled by section 68 of the Solicitors (Amendment) Act 1994 to write to prospective clients after meeting them, setting out their terms of engagement, fees and so on (see Appendix II). This is an important statutory requirement and the Law Society provides their members with a template of letters and forms their members can use to comply with this legislation. If a law firm does not send out such a letter it is in breach of the law.

The new Legal Services Bill will also introduce significant changes to the legal profession. The Bill is currently going through amendments but the outcome, when made into law, will alter some of the ways the legal profession currently operates. Until the Bill finally becomes law, we don't know which provisions in the Bill in their current form will survive. (See Appendix IV.)

Communication – Setting the Ground Rules

At this first meeting, enquire what the solicitor's practice is regarding communication with clients on cases. You will want to avoid weeks or months of no news so this needs to be clarified with your solicitor at the outset. If this is agreed then there won't be a need for endless phone calls seeking to know what is happening. Litigation has certain stages in processing the court documents so explaining the time scales for these should not be a problem.

There should be an agreed arrangement that phone calls or emails will be responded to. There is nothing more frustrating than chasing up a lawyer who does not return phone calls.

You should also raise the query as to what will happen to your case if the solicitor gets involved in another, big, case. This happens, so there needs to be a contingency plan which will meet your needs and not leave your case less prioritised.

You should discuss at this meeting the question of a problem arising between you and your solicitor and what procedures they would recommend to deal with it. Hopefully no problems will arise or if they do they can be cleared up quickly, and if you have a good relationship with your solicitor then it will be resolved. However, in the instance of a serious matter you could enquire whether they would be open to arbitration. Most good solicitors would not oppose this method. However, my experience is that solicitors don't like others looking into how they run their business so if there is a resistance to arbitration they need to have some acceptable procedure in place to deal with the complaint or breakdown in the working relationship.

So many problems arising in the course of working with your solicitor can be resolved by an upfront exchange at the initial meeting and agreeing procedures to deal with any problems arising in the future. You don't want a falling-out with your solicitor, a stand-off with virtually no communication between you and the hassle and additional cost of changing solicitors.

Lastly, you should raise with the solicitor the issue of whether your case will involve briefing a barrister and what that entails for you. A barrister is obliged to give a written estimate of fees prior to undertaking work unless this is impossible due to the urgency of the matter. As most barristers' work involves litigation, this can become complex and hard to genuinely pin down an exact cost.

Clients' 'Do' List

- Do take notes and keep a record of all communications with the solicitor
- Do collect all documents
- Do enquire whether the solicitor has done similar work
- Do discuss fees

Clients' 'Don't' List

- Don't hold back documents or information from the solicitor

- Don't judge your choice of solicitor on fees; the cheapest may not be the best
- Don't leave the initial meeting with unanswered questions

4

Understanding the Relationship between Client and Solicitor

At this juncture you have engaged a solicitor and have confidence in your selection. It is important to see the relationship between you and the solicitor as being part of a team, with the solicitor being the project leader. They will lead the project and will seek to gather all the information that is needed.

It is important to understand the differing roles the parties play. The client will be, understandably, subjective whereas the solicitor must be objective in their work and approach. Solicitors are forensic in their pursuit of relevant information. They cannot proceed with the work until all the relevant information has been obtained. This pursuit of information requested by the solicitor may be a nuisance or inconvenience but they are acting in your best interests and want to avoid any surprises that may surface at a critical time later.

So if your solicitor asks for a list of information they need, be sure to obtain it. Don't be judgmental and decide they won't need this or that.

Remember time is money – your money. If you assemble all the requested information together and bundle it in a folder for the solicitor and let them sort it out it's wasting your money. Take the time to place the documents into sequential order. The solicitor is skilled at ascertaining the legal issues, separating the relevant facts from the irrelevant. The solicitor is not a filing clerk but, if you give them that chore you will be paying their normal hourly rate (expensive clerk!).

In assembling the requested information don't be judgmental yourself in deciding if this email or that letter is of use. Remember the project leader? It is their job to decide what stays in the file and what can be discarded.

Be careful with emails: do a search and print off all the emails from the parties involved. Some email services bundle the emails together so you need to painstakingly read them all so that none are excluded. It is a tedious task but sometimes a critically important detail is found in an innocent-looking email.

Do not delete or destroy any document or email, even if you are certain it contains nothing of interest. In litigation it is common to seek 'discovery orders' and if one is served on you for, say, email correspondence then you have to comply with the order. If the other side, during discovery, finds that an email was deleted (even though you believe it had no value) the court may take the view that evidence was destroyed. Your solicitor will walk you through any discovery procedure but once legal proceedings are initiated, or indeed intended to be issued, destruction of any documents must be avoided. There are software programmes now that make email discovery easier and your solicitor could advise you here.

In the early stages of litigation you will see more of your solicitor as the information is gathered, and here your relationship with your solicitor should deepen as you get to understand each other's needs. If you feel issues are getting complex, ask questions so you stay on top. You, the client, need to be informed and understand what is happening. Solicitors tend to be quite literal in their manner so if you ask a question be specific and clear with your query.

Your solicitor will distinguish between the points in your case – the strong ones and the weak. They may eliminate certain evidence which you may not agree with. They have their reasons but ask why; you need to know and cannot or should not be left in the dark.

It is fine to put your total trust in your solicitor but this does not mean you abandon them to carry the case. You are an important part of the team so be informed and know and understand everything your solicitor is doing on your case – after all it is *your* case.

It is only natural that a client takes a case personally so emotions can run high at times. You may feel a certain line should be taken but your solicitor is reluctant to go with that. They have their reasons. Ask them why. It may be that a certain person may not make a good witness and under cross-examination could in fact harm your case. This is the solicitor acting in the overall best interests of your case. They are being objective and weighing up the pros and cons.

Looking at your case from the familiar surroundings of your office or home may give you confidence of success but on the day in court witnesses are in the cold, unfriendly, almost clinical surroundings of a courtroom and this can unnerve witnesses. Solicitors will, when meeting clients and potential witnesses, weigh up whether they think the person before them will be good witness. This is down to their expertise and judgement. Having a good case on paper is one thing but it has to be delivered in court by oral evidence and if the solicitor has any doubt on this they will take that into consideration on how best to win your case.

You, as the client, need to be rational at critical decision times. There is no room for taking umbrage or seeking revenge on the other party. This could distract from the matter at hand – winning the case. The case will be decided on the law, not on how one feels about the other party.

Here the solicitor will steer you on the right path so be warned to put aside your hostile feelings for revenge.

You may have a good case but good cases can be lost by a nervous witness and good lawyers can win bad cases. If you or one of your witnesses performs poorly in the witness box, the lawyer on the other side will be presented with an opportunity and you can be sure they won't pass on it. So listening to your solicitor here is important. Their advice on how they will present your case in court is based on their expertise; this is their back yard, and this advice should be heeded, not resisted.

The time up to the day in court is all preparation. In the course of this period, issues will arise which may alter the intended plan. Documentary evidence may not stack up as hoped; there may be an inconclusive paper trail; a witness may be deceased or living abroad and you need to decide if it is worth the cost of bringing them back; or a former employee may have since gotten married, changed their name and become untraceable. Evidence of your case needs to be produced in court and it doesn't always pan out the way you first thought. Here you will see your solicitor and barrister at work. As the landscape of your case shifts the lawyer has to respond and chart out the best course for you with the evidence they have to work with.

Clients' 'Do' List

- Do use the time with your solicitor wisely
- Do trust the judgement of your solicitor
- Do ask questions if you don't understand anything
- Do give the solicitor documents in sequential order

Clients' 'Don't' List

- Don't destroy documents
- Don't delete emails
- Don't take short cuts in assembling the information

5

Understanding the System

Appendix I explains the structure of the Irish courts system. However, you also need to understand *how* the system works. Once litigation is initiated the process is controlled by the courts system. It is generally thought that the litigation process is slow. Some believe the system of court vacations contribute to delays. However, the opposite is the case. The system needs breaks to catch up with the paperwork created by the system. Court registrars are sitting in court during hearings but they have non-court work too and need time to get through it.

Judges of the higher courts have a huge workload. Often cases run into days or weeks. They deliver *ex tempore* (oral) judgments to cases they hear on the day. These are at the conclusion of the case and delivered orally. But in longer cases they cannot deliver a judgment on the day with so much evidence to digest and consider so they need the vacation periods to consider the evidence and write up their judgments. On the day or evening preceding a new case they will read the court papers so they have an idea of what the dispute is before the case opens. The High Court delivers in excess of 500 written judgments a year, with the duration of cases running from a day to several weeks and in some instances longer. The High Court has to cover all of the country and goes out to the provinces to hear appeals from the Circuit Courts.

Litigants can understandably become frustrated with delays waiting to get a hearing date due to the congestion of the lists. So it makes sense at the outset to consider whether one of the forms of alternative dispute resolution (ADR) could resolve the disputed matter (see Chapter 8). Nowadays there is greater choice for resolving disputes; ADR can be used for a huge range of cases and can deal with the issues in a time frame where the restraints of our courts system do not get in the way.

The lowest level of the courts system is the District Court, which is a court of local and summary (judge only) jurisdiction. It deals with minor civil and criminal matters, family law and licensing. Above this is the Circuit Court, which deals with more serious civil and criminal matters, and also family law. Ireland is divided into eight circuits: Dublin, Cork, Eastern, Midland, Northern, South-Eastern, South-Western and Western. Barristers become members of a circuit of their choice and travel to the circuit towns where the Circuit Court sits. Circuit barristers ply their business during the week on the circuit and as the Circuit Court usually does not sit on Mondays circuit barristers on that day usually are in Dublin attending cases from their circuit that may be in the High Court.

Cases heard in one court can be appealed to the next higher court, e.g. appeals from the District Court go to the Circuit Court, Circuit Court appeals go to the High Court and High Court appeals go to the Supreme Court.

Solicitors normally operate in the District Court, though for any complex matters barristers can be used; it is very seldom a senior counsel would appear in a District Court. In Circuit Court cases barristers are more commonly used.

The Commercial Court and the Central Criminal Court are divisions of the High Court which exclusively hear commercial and criminal cases respectively. There are also a number of other legal bodies which can hear cases within their specific jurisdiction, such as the Employment Appeals Tribunal, the Equality Tribunal and the Labour Court. Findings from these bodies can be appealed to the Circuit Court.

Clients' 'Do' List

• Do be patient and allow the system to take its course

Clients' 'Don't' List

- Don't dismiss the option to use ADR or go to one of the specialist legal bodies without due consideration

6

Fees

The subject of fees has been touched on earlier but as it is so important it necessitates a closer look.

The subject of fees can become a difficult issue if there is a lack of clarity and the client ends up with a legal bill that takes them by surprise. In today's economic climate, solicitors want to ensure they get paid for their work so will broach the subject themselves at the initial meeting.

The solicitor charges for costs incurred by filing official forms, for example issuing summons and affidavits, but their main fee is for their time, i.e. their expertise.

Some legal services provided by the solicitor may have a standard charge rate, such as for wills or divorce, with a rider for complex matters; or you may agree a fixed rate for the work to be done. Here the solicitor will know from past experience how long the matter will take and can set a fixed fee.

Larger firms will charge by an hourly rate. For firms doing this you need to know the structure of how this works. For example, some firms may charge by the hour with fee time broken into units of four quarters. Here, if a solicitor is speaking to the client for five minutes or fifteen minutes it is billed as one-quarter of the hourly rate. Alternatively, they may bill just the amount of time the conversation actually was, so five minutes would be billed as one-twelfth of the hourly rate. This is information you need to ascertain from the outset.

Hourly rates will differ significantly among law firms and there will be a difference in rates between the larger Dublin firms and provincial firms. Within the firms' rates, they will differ too between partners and junior solicitors. When discussing fees, find out whether additional solicitors will be working on your case and their rates. Check too if solicitors' apprentices will be involved and whether you will be charged for their time and at what rate. Most law firm websites will not give information on their fees so the only way of learning this is to ask questions.

In additional to the above, there are the extra costs known as 'outlay'. This is where you will be billed for photocopying, couriers, phone calls, stamps, etc. You need to ask what the firm's policy on this is. There is, I believe, a case to be made that such outlay should be part of the firm's overhead and the client not be billed for them. Take for instance a situation where a solicitor has an hour-long telephone conversation with the client or on the business of the client with a third party, for which the client will be billed an hour's fee time. But will the client also be charged for the price of the phone call?

As mentioned in Chapter 4, you should give the solicitor the papers on the legal matter you need their assistance on in good order so as to minimise the cost. Equally, you should only phone or communicate with the solicitor when you have something important to discuss. Prior to any such calls make out a list of the matters to be covered. A disorganised client who sends in bits of information and rings up their solicitor on minor matters will chalk up much bigger fees than they need to. The solicitor cannot be blamed for this. Most good solicitors are busy and they too do not want to be wasting their time on unnecessary phone calls. So use your solicitor wisely.

Some solicitors will provide a 'no foal, no fee' service in certain kinds of cases, but they need to be very confident of success before taking on the case. Also, in such instances, you need to learn what exactly you are getting free. In this instance, paying the outlay the solicitor will incur in taking on your case would be reasonable.

Some law firms may offer a fixed fee rate; this gives the client comfort in knowing what they are paying for. However, it would be unlikely this arrangement would apply to litigation, where the unpredictable can add considerable time to a case.

When receiving invoices from your solicitor for services performed you should request a full breakdown of fees and any other costs with a breakdown of items.

If a barrister is brought into a case, the solicitor will first discuss it with you and give the reasons. The solicitor briefs the barrister and discharges their fee so the solicitor will have to have your prior consent to bring in counsel. Here too an estimate of the barrister's fees should be obtained. The Bar Council requires barristers to give an estimate of their fees.

There shouldn't be a mystery as to solicitors' costs and the client should get a bill in line with expectations. This can only be achieved by dealing with the issue at an early stage of engagement.

Clients' 'Do' List

- Do enquire about the system of fee calculation
- Do enquire about additional charges such as outlay
- Do seek itemised invoices

Clients' 'Don't' List

- Don't waste your solicitor's time, this will add to your costs
- Don't judge a solicitor on fees alone
- Don't be unclear on fee issues

7

Working as a Team

Once you engage a solicitor (and possibly a barrister too) to take on your case you are strengthening your team to achieve the result you want. You do not 'hand over' the matter and leave it to the lawyers to solve. The papers and briefing you give the solicitor will inform them of the issues at hand but as the case progresses they will need you to be involved. As a team player, withholding information from your lawyer of a development at your end will not help.

If you are concerned about an approach the lawyer is taking, discuss it with them. Do not let it fester to a point where it is too late to raise the issue or do anything with it. Your lawyer needs to know how you are feeling as progress is made. They won't be offended, or should not be offended, by you asking questions on why they are recommending a particular course of action. There will be a reason why a lawyer is proceeding in a certain way, but you need to understand why and be comfortable with it.

Even if your lawyers are the best in their area, a client's input is coming from a different angle and this can contribute to the outcome of the discussion. If your lawyer is a sole practitioner, this is all the more reason for a second view on the issues.

By working with your lawyer you will understand their personality and approach to issues. This of course could irritate you but at least you can understand how they approach things. It also gives you the opportunity to investigate with your lawyer whether it is the right approach. They will be coming to the problem objectively whereas you, the client, will be subjective and, at times, emotional. The lawyer needs to understand how you are approaching the issues and this can only be understood by working together.

Clients' 'Do' List

- Do give facts
- Do be a team player
- When giving your opinion on facts do clearly state as such
- Do hand over all documentation
- Do organise the documentation in sequential order
- Do keep a record and copies of everything handed over

- Do keep a record of all dealings with legal advisors

Clients' 'Don't' List

- Don't withhold information
- Don't confuse facts with your opinion on facts
- Don't keep your legal advisors in the dark with developments
- Don't be untruthful
- Don't expect miracles; be realistic in your expectations

8

Alternative Dispute Resolution

Alternative dispute resolution, commonly referred to as ADR, is growing in popularity as a means of resolving disputes between parties. It involves training, which many lawyers now have, in techniques for disagreeing parties to come to an agreement that avoids litigation. It is, therefore, an alternative to the traditional route of resorting to the courts.

This form of redress can be used from simple disputes to more complex commercial cases. The procedure is there so it is clearly an alternative worthy of consideration for commercial disputes.

ADR is an umbrella term that encompasses a number of different forms of non-litigious dispute resolution. Two of the most common forms of ADR are arbitration and mediation.

In arbitration a neutral third party, known as an 'arbitrator', imposes a legally binding resolution on the parties involved. Although parties may appeal arbitration outcomes to the court, such appeals face an exacting standard of review.

In mediation the neutral third party, known as a 'mediator', facilitates the resolution process (and may even suggest a resolution, typically known as a 'mediator's proposal') but does not impose a resolution on the parties. The terms of the agreement are decided upon by the parties involved. Generally, decisions made in mediation are not legally binding, unless both parties agree to it.

Arbitration, especially, has always been available but I think there was a preference even among lawyers to take the litigation route rather than arbitration or mediation. But that thinking has changed radically in recent years and you only have to look at law firms' websites to see ADR is often offered as part of their services. An increasing number of lawyers, and indeed other professionals too, are trained in ADR. ADR has gained widespread acceptance among both the general public and the legal profession so a lawyer will not be annoyed if you suggest taking this route as a possibility.

The ADR procedure is more 'friendly' too than the austere surroundings of a courtroom. Litigation lawyers are comfortable in the latter as it is where they work, but litigants can often find the courts intimidating and unnerving. This obviously can have an impact on how they give evidence and could affect the outcome of a case. Think about it. You have spent months, even years, in painstakingly putting your case together and then your day in court arrives. You are out of your comfort zone in the courtroom, in surroundings unfamiliar to you. The dress code and the language are foreign to you. You have a long wait for your case to come up: that wait could be days. The lawyers follow the practice and procedure of the system – a puzzle to the layman. There are last minute changes. Unless you are from another planet this has to unsettle you in some way.

The ADR process is miles away from the litigation process. The third-party arbitrator or mediator is chosen by the parties. The hearing days are agreed and are not confined by any rules or vacation periods. Sitting times are like office hours. It's all very business-like, which allows the parties to relax in a way that is not possible in courtroom litigation.

Litigation through the courts system is slow and one of the contributing reasons for that is the number of cases listed before the courts. ADR can reduce the pressure on the court system while benefiting both litigant and defendant through reduced costs, giving them control over who is the adjudicating party, an informal setting and greater privacy due to the confidentiality of the process.

There is a move that in some proceedings the courts now require parties to try mediation, and only if that fails do they allow the parties' case to be heard in court.

In taking a case to a solicitor litigation may be in your mind but there are other options than just the litigation route. Most litigation cases are settled so it is worth exploring arbitration or mediation before issuing proceedings. Clients have more control over, or input into, the final resolution in mediation than through litigation. Arbitration is similar to litigation except it is done in private and in a more informal atmosphere. It is also faster than litigation as when your case is heard is not dictated by law terms or where your case is 'in the list'.

In arbitration you can still have your solicitor representing you so the process is quite similar to court litigation but there are procedural differences. You can agree with the other side who the arbitrator will be, whereas there is no such control in the courts system. Papers are exchanged between the parties as in the litigation proceeding but the procedure is agreed by the parties. The parties can send in written submissions and the arbitrator makes their ruling without meeting the parties. Or, there can be a hearing with evidence taken.

The ruling of the arbitrator is binding on both parties and consequently enforceable; there are some narrow exceptions to this but generally once you embrace the arbitration route the decision will have the same impact as that of a judge. In mediation the parties themselves come to an agreed resolution. The decision is not legally enforceable unless the parties agree to make it so.

In relation to costs, in typical litigation when a party loses the other side claims that costs follow the event and there is a specific rule of the courts that provides that the party who has failed to succeed with their case is liable for the legal costs of the other side. In arbitration, a typical order with regard to costs would follow what happens in the courts. However, an arbitrator has considerable discretion with regard to how they might award costs.

Your solicitor can advise whether they think an alternative to court litigation is best for your case and this should be raised at the initial meeting as an option.

Arbitration and mediation are growing in popularity and most law firms are engaging in these processes. They are certainly worth exploring to see if they benefit your problem.

Clients' 'Do' List

- Do understand the differences between ADR and litigation before proceeding
- Do carefully consider whether arbitration or mediation would be the better option in your specific circumstances

Clients' 'Don't' List

- Don't dismiss alternative options without considering them
- Don't rush; weigh up which is best for you

9

Negotiations

Whether you engage a solicitor for litigation or ADR, your solicitor will be involved in negotiations at some level. If you are purchasing or disposing of an asset or a service, the agreement that seals the deal will need to be put down on paper. Here your solicitor will be seeking the best terms for you and explaining what obligations, if any, arise under the agreement. This can be tedious work and requires the mind to be objective and focused on achieving the end goal.

Negotiation is the art of persuasion. It is important to discuss with your solicitor in advance the approach they will take in these negotiations, otherwise it could result in an untimely intervention by you during the negotiations, which could undermine the point your solicitor was seeking to make. You need to act as a team.

A well-experienced negotiator will be in control of the talks and in observing their counterpart will employ subtle methods to win over the opposition to their way of thinking.

In negotiations it is interesting to see who is leading the way: are they being too pushy, are they being listened to or resisted by the opposing party? The lawyers do the talking but you, the client, should observe the personalities unwind, take notes, and then at an interval discuss with your solicitor what you are seeing.

There are different techniques in negotiation. A solicitor may at the outset try to develop a rapport with the other side through trivial conversation. If the lawyers know each other already the rapport is already there and could be more conducive to reaching a resolution faster than had they not known each other.

You should agree with your solicitor in advance what concessions you are prepared to make in the negotiations. You solicitor will be aware of these during the talks but will only introduce them or one of them when they believe that by doing so they can get the other side to make a concession. They may hold back until there is a particular concession they want the other party to make so they will bide their time. Their concession therefore becomes an inducement to the other side to concede on their point. Your solicitor in effect is luring their prey into their web.

Another technique would be for your solicitor to seek a substantial concession, knowing it is a big ask and will be declined. On being declined, they then make a more modest request. The object here is to make the other party feel good that your solicitor is willing to climb down on their request and hence make the other side more inclined to concede to the lesser request.

As the client, you need to understand the approaches your solicitor is making or you risk putting your foot in it by saying something that could undermine your solicitor's well-thought-out plan of negotiation.

It is important to know in advance who the negotiators on the other side are. There is always a possibility that a senior solicitor may be on their team. This has to be thought through. You do not want one party taking a dominant role because they are considered a person of authority. So asserting one's position at an early stage in a subtle way could send out the signal to that senior person that they are not controlling the talks.

Skilled negotiators will see through the tricks of negotiation employed by the other party. As the client you should remain quiet and leave matters with your solicitor. You might feel intimidated and worried if the other party offers some concession but adds that there is only a limited time to accept. Your solicitor will understand the nuances of what is happening and play their hand when ready.

The lesson here is be prepared, do your home-work, work out the strategy with your solicitor in advance and trust them to deliver the best result for you.

Clients' 'Do' List

- Do leave negotiations in the control of the professionals
- Do ensure you understand the approach taken
- Do ask questions if you are unsure of anything at this important stage

Clients' 'Don't' List

- Don't undermine the work of your legal advisors

10

Settling Cases

When the possibility of settling your case arises your solicitor will assess the issues and offer practical advice for you to consider. You can then instruct them accordingly. The solicitor will evaluate the risks and from experience give educated guesses on what the likely outcome may be. This would be before a barrister is involved. Usually once a barrister is engaged it is the barrister who will handle settlement negotiations.

All cases have risk, even very strong cases. If the other side know this and realise they have a weak case, the lawyer representing them, while knowing the limitations of their case, will nonetheless act as though they have a good case. So, like a game of poker, there is bluffing and gamesmanship going on and the lawyers know how to play this game. The clients sometimes lose their nerve as the court day nears but their lawyer does not and is there to fight their corner.

As the court day looms, settlement comes into the frame. It is not unusual for the parties' lawyers to have an 'off the record' conversation to sound out the other side. The lawyer with the weaker case may be looking for a way to settle the case and reduce the exposure of their client. On the other side, the stronger party may be interested in hearing what the other party has to say and see if an acceptable settlement can be reached which their client would be happy with. No settlement would be made without the client's agreement.

The party with the weaker case can save on cost exposure by settling the case and avoiding a full hearing with all the related costs. This way the strong party could agree a settlement without having to give away too much and avoid the risk of something going wrong in court.

Settlement negotiations are a skill. As I will discuss in Chapter 11, this is where barristers excel. Solicitors too engage in settlements but barristers, being primarily litigation practitioners, have more experience in this.

During these settlement exchanges the lawyer is constantly weighing up the risks, the advantages and the weak points, and evaluating whether with the changing circumstances they can get a settlement they can take back to you. The lawyer may come back to you and say the other side are offering X and they may add that they believe they can do better so they are advising you to decline. When that point arrives, there will be conflicting thoughts going through your head. You may be relieved and desire avoiding the hearing (hanging around a court can be unnerving) but try to remember the issues – do you believe you have a good case – and decide on the facts and issues of the case and not on how you feel on the day.

In settlement negotiations the lawyers are having a mini-run-through of the case in their exchanges, putting forward your strong points, responding to points made by the other side. Always one party is more eager to settle than the other but they won't let their guard down and will continue to push for their client even though they know they are on weak ground. The skill of settlement negotiation is critical. Your lawyer is earning their fee here. Negotiation skills are honed by experience so it is the home territory of the litigation lawyer – in these parts, mainly barristers.

Before a case gets near a court hearing it is possible that solicitors representing opposing parties to a case will speak and a resolution could emerge from that; as the case nears conclusion with neither party having shown a willingness to settle it is best to leave any settlement negotiations to the experts.

If you and your legal team believe you have a good case it would be better to await an approach from the other side to settle; otherwise it could be interpreted as a sign of weakness in your case. You need to be strong and not be intimidated by any claims by the opposing side. Keep your distance from the other side. Avoid contact if possible and let the lawyers meet away from you. If you are in close proximity to the other side, in a corridor or tea room for example, avoid direct contact, referring them to the lawyers who are handling the matter. If such contact is made, tell your lawyer.

In these situations, the trust you will have built up with your lawyer in the time leading up to the case is vitally important. You must have 100 per cent confidence in your lawyer.

Settlement talks can take time; if they are on the day of the court hearing and the time has come to start the case a judge will often give the parties more time if they believe a settlement can be achieved. An outcome reached by the parties coming to a mutual agreement is much more preferable to a judge having to decide and force a decision on the parties.

In a negotiated settlement, you need to approach the process with a willingness to concede on some points. Your lawyers will advise on what these may be and what will appeal to the other party.

Clients' 'Do' List

- Do trust your lawyer in settlement matters
- Do be prepared to compromise
- Do listen to the advice of your legal team

Clients' 'Don't' List

- Don't make contact with the other side without the knowledge of your legal team
- Don't ignore the advice of your legal team

11

The Role of the Barrister

The legal profession in Ireland is divided into two branches: solicitors and barristers. The solicitor is the public's first contact for their legal problems. If the problem is neither complex nor involving courts at a senior level then the solicitor can handle the matter and it goes no further. But if it is a matter where special expertise is required or which involves the Circuit, High or Supreme Courts, then the engagement of a barrister (or 'counsel') is made (if the client consents to it).

Strictly speaking the client of the barrister is the instructing solicitor, but in effect they are acting for the client with the legal problem. The barrister's fees are discharged by the solicitor on behalf of their client so all financial matters are conducted between the client and the solicitor.

While barristers engage in advisory work they are mainly employed in litigation. Barristers are experts in presenting and arguing cases in court or tribunals.

Barristers are self-employed and under our system a solicitor can access the leading barristers in the country for a client, thereby enabling a small law firm, which may have a case against one of the biggest law firms in the country, to engage a top barrister to even out the playing field.

Barristers draft the court proceedings, prepare legal submissions in writing and present the client's case in court. The solicitor will have gathered the information from the client and prepares a 'brief' for the barrister. The brief sets out the client's case with copies of relevant correspondence. The barrister devises a course of action from the brief and advises the solicitor. They in turn advise the client. In some instances the barrister will advise there is no case and it would be a waste of money to pursue any action. Here the case ends and the client is informed by their solicitor. In other cases it may require the barrister to meet the client for a consultation to ascertain further information. Otherwise, the barrister may feel there is a case to answer and advise accordingly.

Courtroom skills of advocacy are central to a barrister's training. Documentary evidence for court proceedings can be required in evidence but often a case will be won or lost by the oral evidence of witnesses. Here the barrister's skill is best served. A well-argued case can be influential in persuading a judge (or jury) in your favour.

Cross-examination of witnesses by your barrister could destroy or damage their case.

Barristers with specialist skills in court are in a good position to advise on the strengths and weaknesses of their client's case and whether to fight the case or settle it through negotiations. Many of the cases coming before the courts are settled and it is the barrister who can advise you on the best settlement and do the negotiations for you.

Increasingly, barristers are engaged outside the traditional courtroom setting such as in mediations, arbitrations, tribunals and disciplinary hearings.

Barristers are obliged by their professional body (the Bar Council) to give a written estimate of fees prior to undertaking work unless this is impossible due to the urgency of the matter or the work is undertaken under the Civil or Criminal Legal Aid Schemes (under which, in certain cases, the State pays a fee set by the State for the barrister to act for a client in their case).

Obtaining such an estimate will allow you and your solicitor to shop around to ensure that you obtain the best representation in terms of quality and price. Furthermore, the barrister must update the fee estimate as necessary if circumstances change.

Solicitors often have a list of barristers whom they regularly use and with whom they have a good working relationship. However, for cases with a particular specialty solicitors will go outside this list. If a client wants to use a specific barrister that is often agreed to by the solicitor provided they are happy the barrister in question has, in the solicitor's opinion, the experience to deal with the matter.

There is no set scale of fees charged by barristers and the fee is usually negotiated by the solicitor on the client's behalf. The level of any particular fee has to be based upon the work done having regard to the factors mentioned above. Like any profession, the most successful barristers, who are extremely busy, will charge more. The fee is for their time and expertise; there are no extras such as outlay or travel expenses.

The barrister profession has a tradition of ensuring that no one is left without proper representation simply because of their means. In these circumstances they provide services at less than the normal commercial rate or at no cost to the client. In appropriate cases which are not covered by legal aid schemes a barrister may be willing to take on a case on a 'no foal, no fee' basis. This means that the barrister will not require the payment of fees unless the client is successful (in which case the fees are usually ordered by the court to be paid by the other side).

Barristers are either junior or senior counsel. When a barrister commences practice they are junior counsel. A barrister can remain a junior counsel throughout their career or, after ten years or more, they can apply to become a senior counsel, sometimes referred to as a 'silk'. It is a position reserved for barristers of particular ability and experience. About 12 per cent of barristers are senior counsel. Judicial appointments are usually from the senior counsel ranks.

When a solicitor engages a barrister they normally bring in a junior counsel. If, in the opinion of the junior counsel, a senior counsel is required the solicitor will be informed. As this has a cost exposure the client will be consulted before a decision is made. In very complex cases more than one senior counsel may be brought onto a case.

A client may feel they don't need the addition of counsel, preferring the solicitor to represent them from beginning to end. This is of course possible but I would not recommend it. There will be a considerable workload on the solicitor who takes on the dual role of solicitor and the advocacy role of barrister. The courtroom is the workplace of the barrister and they are best placed to speak on behalf of the client there. Also there is the possibility of settlement and this will require good negotiation skills to bring about the best result for the client. Some solicitors would feel up to the challenge but it is a big ask, especially if on the other side there is a team of solicitor and junior and senior counsel.

The work division of senior and junior barristers is that the senior counsel will do most of the advocacy work while the junior will take instructions from the senior and conduct research, case preparation and legal submissions, which are approved by the senior. However, in less complex cases or where the junior counsel is very experienced they will share the advocacy workload.

Clients' 'Do' List

- Do trust the judgement of your solicitor if they believe the engagement of a barrister is necessary
- Do trust the barrister in the same way as your solicitor, they have been specifically chosen by your solicitor for this matter

Clients' 'Don't' List

- Don't take the risk of going without a barrister if your solicitor recommends it
- Don't distance yourself from the engagement of a barrister; they are an addition to your team

12

Trust and Openness

Any relationship needs trust and openness on both sides to work. The client has a problem they cannot resolve themselves and the solicitor has the skill to assist with that problem. The solicitor, once engaged, is on your side.

Some people think that lawyers are too chummy with each other and become suspicious if they see their lawyer talking – or worse, laughing – with an opposing lawyer. Ireland is a small country; the number of places to study to become a solicitor or barrister is two – the Law Society and King's Inns – so it is inevitable that in such a small community lawyers will know each other.

Clients take cases personally, that is not unusual. They feel aggrieved at a contract that was broken or some injury or cost to them caused by another person or company. But the lawyer takes an objective perspective. Lawyer X may represent you and Lawyer Y may represent the other party.

Both may be social or sporting friends. They could play a round of golf together and never mention your case. Why? Well one reason is that they have at any one time dozens of clients' cases at various stages of development but, most importantly, if they are not briefed by you to discuss the case with the other party, they won't – trust. After all, they are probably on the golf course to get away from the clients.

A lawyer is not going to jeopardise their relationship with a client by doing solo runs without discussing it in advance with them. Conversely, a lawyer might ring their client and say they are matched to play golf with the opposing lawyer and ask the client shall they use the opportunity to raise their case and see what happens.

Lawyers act on the instructions of their clients. If they overstep that mark then they are in breach of their instructions and should be dismissed. The client must be informed at all times of contact with the opposing party.

Remember, lawyers act on information supplied to them. As the client, you need to ensure the information supplied is accurate. If you notice an error you should inform the solicitor of the error.

A client withholding information is not a good idea. A client may be embarrassed about some aspect and decide to 'hold back for the moment'. But how can your lawyers advise you if you give incomplete information?

Withholding information may be innocent. A client may subjectively decide 'this is not important' and discard it. Let the lawyer be the judge of what is important and not important.

Clients' 'Do' List

- Do trust your legal team to act in your best interests
- Do consider allowing your lawyer the opportunity to informally discuss your case with the opposing lawyer if they suggest it

Clients' 'Don't' List

- Don't withhold any information from your legal team
- Don't be suspicious if your lawyer is personal friends with the opposing party's lawyer

13

Agreements and Contract Negotiations

All significant commercial transactions, whether it is for the provision of services or sale or acquisition of an asset, will require the deal to be reduced to paper.

The commercial parties may agree to do the deal 'subject to contract'; it is at this stage that a client will need to be professionally advised. There are considerations that those involved in business may not take into account at such times so rushing a deal or paying insufficient attention to detail could have dire consequences.

Some clauses in what appear to be long-winded agreements may be given only a cursory glance, yet if something goes pear-shaped months or years after the conclusion of the contract these clauses could come back and bite if not given due attention.

Most commercial contracts are standard or have become a template from numerous past transactions of the solicitor. So to customise it to suit your particular needs each clause needs to be considered by you and your solicitor to determine whether it stays in or comes out. Insufficient attention to detail or rushing the solicitors to close negotiations could result in a clause or clauses unfavourable to you remaining in the contract.

One of the pitfalls of not paying sufficient attention to the inclusion or exclusion of clauses or understanding them is where two clauses conflict, thus giving an ambiguity to their meaning or interpretation. This could result in a disadvantage to you in the future as once the contracts are signed, that's it.

Tedious as wading through contract clauses line by line is, it is advisable that you do this. If there is any language you do not understand ask your solicitor and be sure you are clear on its meaning. Unfortunately, most of these standard contracts are written in uncommonly used English and with legal jargon. There has been much discussion on removing the legal jargon from such contracts but they are still there and that means we have to deal with them.

Here a solicitor's previous experience in such contracts is vitally important. It's no use to you if you ask your solicitor the meaning of a sentence or clause and there is a delay in their response or you get an 'I think ...'. A delay in their response could mean they themselves are figuring out what it could mean. That is not good enough. For commercial contracts be sure your solicitor has experience in this area.

These negotiations are often dealt with solicitor to solicitor and by post or email exchange. This means the original agreement goes through several versions and it can become very tiresome seeing the same contract with marginal changes from version to version. But it has to be done and here clear instructions to your solicitor will pay its way in spades.

Clients' 'Do' List

- Do pay attention to detail
- Do ask questions if you are uncertain of a clause's interpretation

Clients' 'Don't' List

- Don't skim over versions of a contract expecting 'others' to notice errors

14

Preparation for Court Hearings

Careful preparatory work which has taken months, even years, goes into being ready for your case to be heard in court. Getting documentation and witnesses ready for court is only part of the preparation; getting yourself ready is hugely important. It cannot be overstated how important it is for your head to be clear, your mind focused and you be ready for this important day.

Your solicitor will prepare you for:

- Delays in hearing dates, postponements and hanging around the court area waiting for your case to be called
- Concern over rising costs
- Feeling control slipping away from you
- Concern about giving your own evidence

A good solicitor will ease these pressures and go through how you give your evidence and respond to cross-examination. Remember court work is routine for litigation solicitors and barristers. Often the solicitor will remain with the client, update them on progress – maybe settlement talks are happening – and generally put the client at ease the best they can in the strange clinical surroundings of the courthouse, while the barrister keeps an eye on the lists or is engaged in settlement talks with the other side.

This is the time to keep your nerve. Listen to the advice of your legal team.

If the waiting and the atmosphere of the court area gets to you you could feel pressure to cave in to a settlement. Remember the other side is going through the same pressures; listen to your lawyers and trust the professionals to act in your best interests.

Clients' 'Do' List

- Do listen to the advice of your legal team at this crucial stage
- Do prepare yourself for court

Clients' 'Don't' List

- Don't have a late night before your court day, or drink excessive alcohol
- Don't throw away months of careful preparation by making rash decisions under pressure

15

What to Do if the Relationship with Your Lawyer Breaks Down

If you find your relationship with your solicitor runs into difficulty the best course of action is to try to resolve it between yourself and the solicitor.

Try to identify the cause of the breakdown. If you kept a file on progress, meetings, documents, calls, etc. you can trace the history of your working relationship with your solicitor and use this to your advantage.

The best resolution is to work out a deal with your solicitor so the relationship can continue. Starting with a new solicitor after the process has begun has its complications: finding a replacement solicitor, breaking them in and vice versa, agreeing fees and placing your trust in a new solicitor.

If the dispute involves fees then the information given in Chapter 3 comes to the fore. If you have not nailed down an agreement on fees at an early stage and a dispute arises over them it can become a mess.

If the solicitor feels aggrieved and out of pocket and has papers or property belonging to the client in certain circumstances they can refuse to hand them over until the fees are paid.

The Law Society has procedures for complaints against solicitors; it is the regulatory body for solicitors. The Law Society can investigate complaints against its members by clients on:

- Inadequate professional services
- Excessive fees (there is a time limit of five years). There is also the option, within a year of delivery of the bill, of referring the bill to the Taxing Master (who assesses fees as to their reasonableness).
- Misconduct

Full information can be found on the Law Society's website (www.lawsociety.ie).

The Legal Services Bill, when enacted, will deal with complaints. In its current form, Part 5 of the proposed law deals with 'Complaints and Disciplinary Hearings in Respect of Legal Practitioners' (see Appendix IV). When the Bill becomes law it should be consulted to see your rights.

Until the Legal Services Bill becomes law, for complaints against barristers the first action is to discuss it with your solicitor. Ideally the solicitor will raise it with the barrister and between them the matter will be sorted. However, if that fails the complaint should be directed to the secretary of the Professional Conduct Tribunal of the Bar Council of Ireland. Contact details are on its website (www.barcouncil.ie). Complaints should be made within a reasonable time.

Examples of grounds of complaint include:

- Misconduct
- Breach of confidentiality
- Failing to adhere to proper professional standards
- Acting contrary to instructions
- Being the cause of unjustified delays
- Bullying

Every effort should be made to resolve the subject matter of your complaint to avoid further delay, cost and stress, and only if that fails should you take your complaint to the relevant professional body.

At the time of writing, the Legal Services Bill is making its way through the Oireachtas and amendments will be made before it becomes law so until that happens there is some uncertainty as to what provisions will go and what will remain. In its current form there is provision to radically change the procedure as to how complaints against members of the legal profession will be handled. See Appendix IV for the current proposals. It is proposed that a Legal Services Regulatory

Authority will be established, and this independent body will handle complaints.

Clients' 'Do' List

- Do talk to your solicitor
- Do identify the cause of the breakdown

Clients' 'Don't' List

- Don't get into a stand-off situation
- Don't do nothing

Appendix I

The Courts

Supreme Court

The Supreme Court is the court of final appeal in Ireland. It sits in the Four Courts in Dublin.

Composition of the Court

The Supreme Court is made up of the President of the Court (the Chief Justice) and seven ordinary judges. The President of the High Court is also *ex officio* (because of his/her office) an additional judge of the court. Where one of the ordinary judges of the Supreme Court is President of the Law Reform Commission the number of ordinary judges may be increased by one. Under section 5 of the Courts (No. 2) Act 1997 the number of judges may also be exceeded by one where a former Chief Justice serves as a judge of the Supreme Court. Additionally, where, because of the illness of a judge of the Supreme Court, or for any other reason, an insufficient number of judges of the Supreme Court is available for the transaction of the business of the court the Chief Justice may request any ordinary judge or judges of the High Court to sit as a member of the Supreme Court for the hearing of a matter. Any judge so requested is then an additional member of the court for that hearing.

For procedural appeals or cases which do not involve major legal issues the court would normally consist of three judges. In cases where the constitutionality of a statute is challenged or where important issues of law arise a court of five judges will sit. Seven judges may sit to hear cases of exceptional importance, such as the reference of a Bill to the court under Article 26 of the Constitution.

The Supreme Court may sit in two or more divisions at the same time.

The Chief Justice

Apart from sitting as a member of the Supreme Court, the Chief Justice also sits alone to deal with applications for the appointment of Notaries Public and Commissioners for Oaths and in an administrative capacity for case management lists. The Chief Justice is also *ex officio* an additional judge of the High Court.

Matters Dealt With

The main business of the court is to hear appeals from decisions of the High Court in proceedings that were commenced in the High Court. The court also deals with matters referred to it by way of case stated from a judge of the Circuit Court or of the High Court. This can occur where a question of law arises in the lower court which the parties (or one of them) request should be submitted to the Supreme Court for its opinion. An appeal can also be brought to the Supreme Court from a decision of the Court of Criminal Appeal. Such an appeal can, however, only be brought where the Court of Criminal Appeal itself, or the Attorney General or Director of Public Prosecutions certifies that its decision involves a point of law of exceptional public importance and that it is desirable, in the public interest, that an appeal should be taken to the Supreme Court on that point of law. In addition, section 34 of the Criminal Procedure Act 1967 provides that where, on a question on law, a verdict in favour of an accused person is found by direction of the trial judge, the Attorney General may, without prejudice to the verdict in favour of the accused, refer the question of law to the Supreme Court for determination.

The right of appeal to the Supreme Court from the Central Criminal Court was abolished by section 11 of the Criminal Procedure Act 1993 except for a reference by the Attorney General of a question of law under section 34 of the Criminal Procedure Act 1967 or in so far as the decision of the Central Criminal Court relates to the validity of any law having regard to the provisions of the Constitution.

In addition to its appellate jurisdiction, the Supreme Court also has some original jurisdiction under the Constitution. Article 12 of the Constitution provides that only the Supreme Court, consisting of not less than five judges, can establish whether the President of Ireland has become permanently incapacitated. Article 26 provides for a reference to the Supreme Court by the President (after consultation with the Council of State) of Bills of the type prescribed in the section for a decision as to whether any such Bill or specified provision or provisions of the Bill is or are repugnant to the Constitution.

Hearing of Appeals

Except in very exceptional cases the Supreme Court does not hear the evidence of witnesses. Appeals are heard on the basis of the documents that were before the lower court and a transcript of the oral evidence (where available) or, failing that, on counsel's agreed note of the evidence as approved by the trial judge.

Listing of Appeals

With the exception of urgent appeals which have been given priority, appeals are listed for hearing in the order in which they become ready for hearing. When all necessary books of appeal have been lodged in the Supreme Court Office and the appellant has certified that the appeal is ready for hearing the appeal is included in a list of cases to be allocated dates according to the date of lodgement of the certificate of readiness. Dates are allocated each legal term for the following term in consultation with the Chief Justice. Application may be made to the Chief Justice to allocate a priority hearing date in cases where exceptional urgency or importance can be shown.

Pronouncements of Decisions

Occasionally, the decision of the court is given directly following the hearing of an appeal in an *ex tempore* judgment. More frequently, however, because of the complexity of the issues involved, the court reserves its judgment to give full consideration to the matters raised in the hearing and the legal authorities cited. The court then delivers a considered written judgment at a later date, of which the parties are notified in advance.

The decision of the Supreme Court is that of the majority; although each judge may deliver a separate judgment whether assenting or dissenting. The exception to this principle arises in the case of a decision by the Supreme Court on a question as to the validity of a law having regard to the provisions of the Constitution. In such a case the Constitution provides that the decision shall be pronounced by such judge as the court shall direct and that no other opinion on such question shall be pronounced nor shall the existence of any such other opinion be disclosed. A similar provision applies in the case of a reference of a Bill by the President under Article 26 of the Constitution.

Hearings

The Constitution provides that justice shall be administered in public save in such special and limited cases as may be prescribed by law. Supreme Court sittings in the vast majority of cases are therefore open to the public. The main exceptions are family law and Succession Act cases.

High Court

The High Court consists of the President and thirty-six ordinary judges. The President of the Circuit Court and the Chief Justice are, by virtue of their office, additional judges of the High Court. The High Court has full jurisdiction in and power to determine all matters and questions whether of law or fact, civil or criminal. Its jurisdiction also extends to the question of the validity of any law having regard to the Constitution. The High Court acts as an appeal court from the Circuit Court in civil matters. It has power to review the decisions of certain tribunals. It may also give rulings on questions of law submitted by the District Court. A person granted bail in the District

Court may apply to the High Court to vary the conditions of bail. If the District Court refuses bail, application may be made to the High Court. A person charged with murder can only apply to the High Court for bail. The High Court exercising its criminal jurisdiction is known as the Central Criminal Court.

The High Court sits in Dublin to hear original actions. It also hears personal injury and fatal injury actions in several provincial locations (Cork, Galway, Limerick, Waterford, Sligo, Dundalk, Kilkenny and Ennis), at specified times during the year. In addition, the High Court sits in provincial venues to hear appeals from the Circuit Court in civil and family law matters.

Matters coming before the High Court are normally heard and determined by one judge but the President of the High Court may decide that any cause or matter or any part thereof may be heard by three judges in what is known as a divisional court.

Circuit Court

The Circuit Court consists of the President and thirty-seven ordinary judges. The President of the District Court is, by virtue of their office, an additional judge of the Circuit Court. The country is divided into eight circuits with one judge assigned to each circuit except in Dublin, where ten judges may be assigned, and Cork, where there is provision for three judges. There are twenty-six Circuit Court Offices throughout Ireland with a County Registrar in charge of the work of each office. The Circuit Court is a court of limited and local jurisdiction. The work can be divided into four main areas: civil, criminal, family law and jury service. The Circuit Court sits in venues in each circuit. Sittings vary in length from one day to three weeks and are generally held every two to four months in each venue in the circuit. Dublin and Cork have continual sittings throughout each legal term.

Civil Business

The civil jurisdiction of the Circuit Court is a limited one unless all parties to an action consent, in which event the jurisdiction is unlimited. The limit of the court's jurisdiction relates mainly to actions where the claim does not exceed €38,092.14 and the rateable valuation of land does not exceed €252.95.

Family Law

The Circuit and High Court have concurrent jurisdiction in the area of family law. The Circuit Court has jurisdiction in a wide range of family law proceedings (judicial separation, divorce, nullity and appeals from the District Court). In hearing such cases the Circuit Court has jurisdiction to make related orders, including custody and access orders and maintenance and barring orders. Applications for protection and barring orders may also be made directly to the Circuit Court. Applications to dispense with the three-month notice period of marriage are also dealt with by the Circuit Court.

Criminal

In criminal matters the Circuit Court has the same jurisdiction as the Central Criminal Court in all indictable offences except murder, rape, aggravated sexual assault, treason, piracy and related offences. This jurisdiction is exercisable in the area where the offence has been committed or where the accused person has been arrested or resides. However, in Circuit Courts outside Dublin the trial judge may transfer a trial to the Dublin Circuit Criminal Court on application by the prosecution or the defence and if satisfied that it would be unjust not to do so. Criminal cases dealt with by the Circuit Criminal Court begin in the District Court and are sent forward to the Circuit Court for trial or sentencing. Where a person is sent forward to the Circuit Criminal Court for trial the case is heard by judge and jury although a person can change their plea to guilty and dispense with a trial. Indictable offences of a minor nature are heard in the District Court where the accused person consents.

Jury Selection

Responsibility for jury selection for the Circuit Criminal Courts rests with the County Registrar in each of the twenty-six counties. Juries for the Central Criminal Court and the High Court are called in Dublin. The Jury Office attached to the Dublin Circuit Court Office is responsible for calling juries for the Dublin Circuit Criminal Court, the Central Criminal Court and certain civil actions, such as defamation, assault and false imprisonment in the High Court.

Appeals from the District Court

Decisions of the District Court can be appealed to the Circuit Court with some exceptions. Appeals proceed by way of a full rehearing and the decision of the Circuit Court is final.

The Circuit Court also acts as an appeal court for appeals from the decisions of the Labour Court and the Employment Appeals Tribunal.

District Court

The District Court consists of a President and sixty-three ordinary judges. The country is divided into twenty-four districts with one or more judges permanently assigned to each district and the Dublin Metropolitan District. Generally the venue at which a case is heard depends on where an offence was committed or where the defendant resides or carries on business or was arrested. Each District Court Office (with the exception of the Dublin Metropolitan District Court) deals with all elements of the work of the District Court. The District Court is a court of local and summary jurisdiction. The business of the District Court can be divided into four categories: criminal, civil, family law and licensing. The District Court has a limited appellate jurisdiction in respect of decisions made by statutory bodies and in these appeals the decision of the District Court is final except where a point of law is at issue. In such instances an appeal can be taken to the High Court. The District Court also deals with miscellaneous actions such as actions taken under the Control of Dogs Acts, applications for citizenship, applications to amend birth and marriage certificates and applications under the Environmental Protection Act 1992 for orders in connection with noise reduction.

Civil Business

The civil jurisdiction of the District Court in contract and most other matters is where the claim or award does not exceed €6,348.69.

Criminal Business

The District Court exercising its criminal jurisdiction deals with four particular types of offences.

Summary offences – these are offences for which there is no right of trial by judge and jury. This makes up the bulk of the criminal work of the District Court; these offences are exclusively statutory in origin.

Indictable offences tried summarily – with the consent of the accused and the DPP and the judge being of the opinion that the facts constitute a minor offence.

Indictable offences – other than certain offences including rape, aggravated sexual assault, murder, treason and piracy where the accused pleads guilty and the DPP consents, and the judge accepts the guilty plea. Otherwise, the accused is sent forward to the Circuit Court on his signed plea of guilty for sentencing.

Indictable offences not tried summarily. With regard to these offences, a Book of Evidence is served on the accused. The judge considers the Book of Evidence and any submissions on behalf of the defence or the prosecution. If the judge is of the opinion that there is a sufficient case to answer, the accused is sent forward to the Circuit Court or Central Criminal Court for trial.

Family Law

The District Court has a wide jurisdiction in the family law area. Proceedings are not heard in open court and are as informal as is practicable.

Domestic Violence

Under the Domestic Violence Act 1996, there are two main types of remedies – safety orders and barring orders.

Guardianship of Children

Under the Guardianship of Infants Act 1964, as amended by the Status of Children Act 1987, the District Court can make custody and access orders and appoint guardians. It also has jurisdiction to establish paternity in relation to any child, with regard to an application for custody, access or maintenance.

Maintenance

Under the Maintenance of Spouses and Children Act 1976 (as amended) the District Court can award maintenance to a spouse and child(ren). The maximum that can be awarded to a spouse is €500 per week and for a child €150 per week. To enforce the order the court can direct that all payments be paid through the District Court Office, make attachment of earnings or issue a warrant for the arrest of the defaulting debtor.

Child Care

Under the Child Care Act 1991, health boards [now the HSE] can make a number of applications to court for orders.

Licensing

The District Court also has wide powers in relation to liquor and lottery licensing.

Reproduced by kind permission of the Courts Services, more information at www.courts.ie.

Appendix II

Section 68 of the Solicitors (Amendment) Act 1994

Charges to clients. **68.**—(1) On the taking of instructions to provide legal services to a client, or as soon as is practicable thereafter, a solicitor shall provide the client with particulars in writing of—

(*a*) the actual charges, or

(*b*) where the provision of particulars of the actual charges is not in the circumstances possible or practicable, an estimate (as near as may be) of the charges, or

(*c*) where the provision of particulars of the actual charges or an estimate of such charges is not in the circumstances possible or practicable, the basis on which the charges are to be made,

by that solicitor or his firm for the provision of such legal services and, where those legal services involve contentious business, with particulars in writing of the circumstances in which the client may be required to pay costs to any other party or parties and the circumstances, if any, in which the client's liability to meet the charges which will be made by the solicitor of that client for those services will not be fully discharged by the amount, if any, of the costs recovered in the contentious business from any other party or parties (or any insurers of such party or parties).

(2) A solicitor shall not act for a client in connection with any contentious business (not being in connection with proceedings seeking only to recover a debt or liquidated demand) on the basis that all or any part of the charges to the client are to be calculated as a specified percentage or proportion of any damages or other moneys that may be or may become payable to the client, and any charges made in contravention of this subsection shall be unenforceable in any action taken against that client to recover such charges.

(3) A solicitor shall not deduct or appropriate any amount in respect of all or any part of his charges from the amount of any damages or other moneys that become payable to a client of that solicitor arising out of any contentious business carried out on behalf of that client by that solicitor.

(4) *Subsection (3)* of this section shall not operate to prevent a solicitor from agreeing with a client at any time that an amount on account of charges shall be paid to him out of any damages or other moneys that may be or may become payable to that client arising out of any contentious business carried out on behalf of that client by that solicitor or his firm.

(5) Any agreement under *subsection (4)* of this section shall not be enforceable against a client of a solicitor unless such agreement is in writing and includes an estimate (as near as may be) of what the solicitor reasonably believes might be recoverable from any other party or parties (or any insurers of such party or parties) in respect of that solicitor's charges in the event of that client recovering any damages or other moneys arising out of such contentious business.

(6) Notwithstanding any other legal provision to that effect a solicitor shall show on a bill of costs to be furnished to the client, as soon as practicable after the conclusion of any contentious business carried out by him on behalf of that client—

(a) a summary of the legal services provided to the client in connection with such contentious business,

(b) the total amount of damages or other moneys recovered by the client arising out of such contentious business, and

(c) details of all or any part of the charges which have been recovered by that solicitor on behalf of that client from any other party or parties (or any insurers of such party or parties),

and that bill of costs shall show separately the amounts in respect of fees, outlays, disbursements and expenses incurred or arising in connection with the provision of such legal services.

(7) Nothing in this section shall prevent any person from exercising any existing right in law to require a solicitor to submit a bill of costs for taxation, whether on a party and party basis or on a solicitor and own client basis, or shall limit the rights of any person or the Society under *section 9* of this Act.

(8) Where a solicitor has issued a bill of costs to a client in respect of the provision of legal services and the client disputes the amount (or any part thereof) of that bill of costs, the solicitor shall—

(a) take all appropriate steps to resolve the matter by agreement with the client, and

(b) inform the client in writing of—

(i) the client's right to require the solicitor to submit the bill of costs or any part thereof to a Taxing Master of the High Court for taxation on a solicitor and own client basis, and

(ii) the client's right to make a complaint to the Society under *section 9* of this Act that he has been issued with a bill of costs that he claims to be excessive.

(9) In this section "*charges*" includes fees, outlays, disbursements and expenses.

(10) The provisions of this section shall apply notwithstanding the provisions of the Attorneys and Solicitors (Ireland) Act, 1849 and the Attorneys and Solicitors Act, 1870.

Appendix III

Periods of Limitation

Every effort has been made to ensure that the information given in this table is accurate. No legal responsibility, however, is accepted for any errors or omissions in this information.

NOTE:

It is important to note that the mere issue of an originating summons may not prevent time from running against the plaintiff, nor prevent an action from being struck out for delay.

Common Types of Action

The effect of the general provisions of section 49 of the Statute of Limitations is that time would not begin to run against a person under a disability (a minor or a person of unsound mind) until such person ceases to be under a disability. Section 49 has been amended by section 5 of the 1991 Act. See also the provisions of the 2000 Act.

Nature of Claim	Time	Statute
Action surviving against estate of deceased person	2 years or relevant period under applicable Statute of Limitations whichever is less	Civil Liability Act 1961, section 9
Action for contribution against concurrent wrongdoers	2 years after ascertainment of liability of claimant or after payment of damages to the injured party or the same period as the injured party is allowed for suing contributor, whichever is greater	Civil Liability Act 1961, section 31

(Continued)

Common Types of Action: (*Continued*)

Nature of Claim	Time	Statute
Personal injuries from negligence, nuisance or breach of duty	Where the relevant date is before 31 March 2005, 3 years from the relevant date or 2 years from 31 March 2005, whichever is lesser. Where the relevant date is on or after 31 March 2005, 2 years Relevant date means the date of accrual of the cause of action or the date of knowledge of the person concerned as respects that cause of action, whichever occurs later	Statute of Limitations (Amendment) Act 1991, section 3(1), as amended by Civil Liability and Courts Act 2004, section 7
Action for damages by or for dependants of person fatally injured	Where the relevant date was before 31 March 2005, 3 years from the relevant date or 2 years from 31 March 2005, whichever is less Where the relevant date is on or after 31 March 2005, 2 years	Statute of Limitations (Amendment) Act 1991, section 6(1), as amended by Civil Liability and Courts Act 2004, section 7

(*Continued*)

95

Common Types of Action: (*Continued*)

Nature of Claim	Time	Statute
Defamation – within the meaning	1 year – or such longer period as the court may direct but not exceeding 2 years from the date on which the cause of action accrued	Statute of Limitations 1957, section 11(2)(*c*) as substituted by the Defamation Act 2009 s.38(1) of the Defamation Act 2009 (No. 31 of 2009) with effect from January 1, 2010 (S.I. No. 517 of 2009) See also section 11(3A) and (3B) as inserted by s.38(1) of the Defamation Act 2009
Airlines – action for personal injury while on board an aircraft or while embarking or disembarking	2 years	Warsaw Convention 1929, Hague Protocol 1955, Montreal Protocol No 4 1975, section 17 Air Navigation Transport Act 1936, section 7 Air Navigation Act 1959 and sections 4 and 7 of the Air Navigation and Transport (International Convention) Act 2004

(Continued)

Common Types of Action: (*Continued*)

Nature of Claim	Time	Statute
Marine – action for damage to a vessel, to cargo or for loss of life or personal injury on board a vessel	2 years	Civil Liability Act 1961, section 46(2)
Simple contract	2 years	Statute of Limitations 1957, section 11
Action for damages under Liability for Defective Products Act 1991	3 years – from date action accrued or date on which plaintiff became aware of damage, defect and identity of producer	Liability for Defective Products Act 1991, section 7
Tort generally other than above	6 years	Statute of Limitations 1957, section 11
Account	6 years	Statute of Limitations 1957, section 11
Interest on judgment	6 years	Statute of Limitations 1957, section 11

(Continued)

Common Types of Action: (*Continued*)

Nature of Claim	Time	Statute
Enforcement of Arbitration Award when arbitration agreement not under seal or where arbitration is under act other than Arbitration Act 1954	6 years	Statute of Limitations 1957, sections 11 and 75–77 (amended by s.29 and Schedule 6 of the Arbitration Act 2010) and Arbitration Act 1954 section 42
Enforcement of Arbitration Award when arbitration agreement under seal	12 years	Statute of Limitations 1957, sections 11 and 75–77 (amended by s.29 and Schedule 6 of the Arbitration Act 2010) and Arbitration Act 1954, section 42
Application set aside an Arbitration Award	Within 3 months of the award being by the party making the application or if made on the grounds of public policy within 56 days of the date the circumstances became known to the party	Article 34 of the UNCITRAL Model Law on International Commercial Arbitration as adopted by the Arbitration Act 2010 and s.12 of the Arbitration Act 2010. Also Rules of the Superior Courts 1986–2010 Order 56 as substituted by S.I. 361 of 2010 Rules of the Superior Courts (Arbitration) 2010

(*Continued*)

Common Types of Action: (*Continued*)

Nature of Claim	Time	Statute
Arrears of rent charge or damages in respect thereof	6 years	Statute of Limitations 1957, section 27
Arrears of rent	6 years	Statute of Limitations 1957, section 28
Arrears of mortgage interest	6 years	Statute of Limitations 1957, section 37
Breach of trust (in absence of fraud or of retention or conversion of trust property) not being an action for which a period of limitation is fixed by any other provision of the act	6 years	Statute of Limitations 1957, section 43
In respect of future interests in trust property right of action deemed not to have accrued until interest falls into possession	None	Statute of Limitations 1957, section 44

(Continued)

Common Types of Action: (*Continued*)

Nature of Claim	Time	Statute
No period of limitation shall apply to an action against a trustee on a claim founded on fraud or fraudulent breach of trust	None	Statute of Limitations 1957, section 44
Claim by beneficiary to estate founded on fraud	6 years	Statute of Limitations 1957, section 45, as deceased not replaced by Succession Act 1965, section 126
Claim by personal representative for recovery of asset on behalf of estate of deceased	12 years	Statute of Limitations 1957, section 13(2); Succession Act 1965, section 126
Arrears of interest in respect of any legacy or damages in respect of such arrears	3 years	Succession Act 1965, section 126
Action on a judgment	12 years	Statute of Limitations 1957, section 11

(Continued)

Common Types of Action: (*Continued*)

Nature of Claim	Time	Statute
Instrument under seal (save for arrears of rent, rent charge, mortgage, arrears of annuity charged on personal property)	12 years	Statute of Limitations 1957, section 11
Recovery of land (other than by State)	12 years	Statute of Limitations 1957, section 13
Recovery of land by State	30 years	Statute of Limitations 1957, section 13
Sale by mortgage	12 years	Statute of Limitations 1957, section 32 A definition of "judgment mortgage" is substituted by s.8(1)and Sch.1 of the Land and Conveyancing Law Reform Act 2009 with effect from 1st December 2009 (S.I. No.356 of 2009)
Recovery of principal monies secured by mortgage	12 years	Statute of Limitations 1957, section 36
Ownership of rent charge	12 years	Statute of Limitations 1957, section 24

References to Amendments to Statute of Limitations 1957

Section in 1957 Act	Effect of Amendment	Amending Provision
Section 2(1)	Amended	Definition of "judgment mortgage" substituted by s.8(1) and Sch.1 of the Land and Conveyancing Law Reform Act 2009
Section 2(2)(c)	Repealed	Registration of Title Act 1964, Sch. but see section 122
Section 2(2)(d)	Repealed	Succession Act 1965 Schedule 2 part IV but see Succession Act 1965 section 123
Section 2(3), 11(1)(e) (iii) and 11(3)	Repealed	Civil Liability Act 1961 Sch. part V
Section 11(2)	Amended	Statute of Limitations (Amendment) Act 1991 section 3, and section 13(8) Sale of Goods and Supply of Services Act 1980
Section 11(2)(c)	Amended	Subsection (2)(c) substituted by s.38(1) of the Defamation Act 2009
Section 11(3A) & (3B)	Inserted	Subsections (3A) and (3B) inserted by s.38(1) of the Defamation Act 2009
Section 11(7)	Applied	Credit Union Act 1966, section 11(10)
Section 21	Amended	Succession Act 1965 Schedule 2 part IV

(Continued)

References to Amendments to Statute of Limitations 1957: (*Continued*)

Section in 1957 Act	Effect of Amendment	Amending Provision
Section 22	Repealed	Succession Act 1965 second schedule
Section 24	Amended	Registration of Title Act 1964, section 49(4)
Section 25(4)	Amended	s.8(1) and Sch. 1 of the Land and Conveyancing Law Reform Act 2009
Section 45	Repealed and amended	Succession Act 1965, section 126 and Sch. 2 part IV
Section 46	Repealed	Succession Act 1965 second schedule
Section 48A	Inserted	Statute of Limitations Amendment Act 2000
Section 49(2)	Repealed	Statute of Limitations (Amendment) Act 1991
Section 49(3)	Amended	substituted by s.38(2) of the Defamation Act 2009
Section 49(4)(*a*)	Repealed	Civil Liability (Amendment) Act 1964 schedule
Section 74	Substituted	s.7(2) of the Arbitration Act 2010
Whole Act	Applied	Registration of Title Act 1964, section 49(1)

Landlord and Tenant Act 1971

Action	Time	Section
Application for sporting lease	Not earlier than 15 years before expiration of current lease and not later than the expiration of the lease or the expiration of three months from the service on the club by its immediate lessor or any superior lessor of notice of expiration of the lease whichever is later. Notice by lessor must be served not earlier than 3 months before expiration of lease	Landlord and Tenant (Amendment) Act, 1971 section 3

Landlord and Tenant (Amendment) Act 1980

(The following list of periods of limitation may not be exhaustive)

Service of notice of intention to claim relief

Action	Time	Section
i. In the case of tenancy terminating by expiration of a term of years or other certain period or event	Before the termination of tenancy or at any time thereafter but before the expiration of three months after service on claimant by landlord of notice of expiration of the term or period of the happening of the event	Section 20
ii. In the case of a tenancy terminating by fall of a life or uncertain event	At any time but before the expiration of three months after service on claimant by landlord of notice of the happening of the event	
iii. In the case of tenancy determined by notice to quit (other than tenancies to which sections 14 or 15 applies)	At any time but before the expiration of three months after service on claimant by landlord of notice to quit	
iv. In the case of tenancy determinable by notice to quit and to which sections 14 or 15 applies	At any time but before the expiration of six months after service on claimant by landlord of notice to quit	

(Continued)

Landlord and Tenant (Amendment) Act 1980: (*Continued*)

Action	Time	Section
Application for reversionary lease	Not earlier than 15 years before expiration of existing lease and not later than the expiration of the lease or 3 months from service of notice by superior lessor, whichever is the later. The notice must be served not earlier than 3 months before the expiration of the lease	Section 31
Improvement notice	Where a tenant proposes to make an improvement, notice must be served on the landlord. The landlord may within one month serve on the tenant a consent or an undertaking to execute the improvement in consideration of an increase in rent to be agreed or fixed by the court or an improvement objection	Section 48
Notice to superior landlord of improvement notice served on landlord	The landlord must within one week serve a notice on his superior landlord, if any	Section 48
Objection to improvements	Landlord must object within one month. Tenant can then apply to court	Section 48 and section 52

(*Continued*)

Landlord and Tenant (Amendment) Act 1980: (*Continued*)

Action	Time	Section
Claim for compensation for improvements	Notice of intention to claim must be made in same period as notice of intention to claim relief – see section 20	Section 56
Compensation on termination of tenancy in obsolete buildings	Landlord must give six months' notice	Section 60
Extension of time	The court may extend time in any proper case	Section 83
Offer of new tenancy in lieu of compensation for improvements	Within 2 months of tenant serving notice to claim compensation for improvements under Part IV	Section 22(1)
Notice accepting new tenancy	Within one month of notice of offer of new tenancy	Section 22(2)
To seek a new tenancy in Custom House Docks area – occupation under certain leases not to be regarded as occupation	Leases which commence during the period of 15 years from passing of Landlord and Tenant (Amendment) Act 1989	Section 13(4) of Landlord and Tenant Amendment Act 1980 as amended by section 1 of Landlord and Tenant Act 1989 and S.I. No. 36 of 1994 and S.I. No. 52 of 1999

Note: Landlord and Tenant (Amendment) Act 1994

Amends the following sections of the 1980 Landlord and Tenant Act

S.3 1994 Act amends s.13 1980 Act:

Paragraph (*a*) of s.13(1) of 1980 Act is amended by the substitution of "5 years" for "3 years"

This shall have effect only in relation to a lease or other contract of tenancy the term of which commences after the commencement of this Act

S.4 amends s.17 of 1980 Act

S.5 amends s.23 of 1980 Act

S.6 amends s.85 of 1980 Act

Landlord and Tenant (Amendment) Act 1984

Action	Time	Section
Notice of intention to review rent in reversionary lease where the terms of such lease are settled by the court under Part III of the 1980 Act	Where the rent has not previously been reviewed, not earlier than one month before the fifth anniversary of the date on which the terms of the lease were settled. Where the rent has been reviewed previously, not earlier than the fifth anniversary of the date of service of the notice for preceding review	Section 3
Application to review the rent of a reversionary lease in default of agreement	Not earlier than one month after the service of the notice	Section 3
Notice of intention to review rent of sporting lease	Same as for reversionary lease	Section 5

(*Continued*)

Landlord and Tenant (Amendment) Act 1984:
(*Continued*)

Action	Time	Section
Application to the court for review of the rent of a sporting lease	Same as for reversionary lease	Section 5
Notice of intention to review rent where the terms of a new tenancy are fixed by the court under Part II of the Landlord and Tenant (Amendment) Act 1980	Same as for reversionary leases and sporting leases	Section 15

Note

The attention of practitioners is also drawn to the provisions as to the acquisition of the fee simple contained in the above Act and to the temporary provisions of the Act at sections 4 and 13 dealing with the right to a reversionary lease and the right to acquire the fee simple in certain cases.

NOTE: RESIDENTIAL TENANCIES ACT 2004

The Residential Tenancies Act 2004 was commenced on the 1st September 2004. Subject to exceptions, the Residential Tenancies Act 2004 applies to every dwelling that is the subject of a tenancy. Among the exceptions to the Act, section 3 excludes a dwelling that is used wholly or partly for the purpose of carrying on a business, formerly rent controlled and long occupation lease tenancies and holiday lettings. Section 100 of the Housing (Miscellaneous) Provisions Act 2009 amends section 3 of the Residential Tenancies Act 2004 to further exclude tenancies for a term longer than 35 years from the provisions of the Act.

Section 192 of the Act abolishes, 5 years after the commencement of Part 4 of the Act, the entitlement to apply, for the first time for a long occupation lease under the Landlord and Tenant (Amendment) Act 1980, except where the tenant has served notice on the landlord of his/her intention to claim that lease under section 20 of the 1980 Act.

Section 191 of the Act amends section 17(1)(*a*) and section 85 of the 1980 Act to permit a tenant to renounce his/her right to a long occupation equity lease under section 13(1)(*b*) of that Act. These sections are further amended by Part 4 of the Civil Law (Miscellaneous Provisions) Act 2008.

Part 4 of the Act provides for security of tenure on the basis of four-year cycles whereby tenancies are deemed terminated at the end of each four-year period and a new tenancy will come into being, assuming that the dwelling continues to be let to the same person(s). During the first six months of each tenancy, the landlord may terminate without giving a reason. During the remaining 3.5 years, termination is only possible where one of the grounds in section 34 of the Act applies. Subject to any fixed term agreement, the tenant will be free to terminate at any time.

Part 5 of the Act specifies the procedures to be followed in terminating a valid tenancy. Termination must be by way of a termination notice regardless of the reason for termination. It provides for gradated notice periods that are linked to the duration of the tenancy (see the tables to section 66, Table 1 applies to landlords and Table 2 applies to tenants).

Part 6 of the Act provides for a mechanism for the resolution of disputes between landlords and tenants of dwellings to which the Act applies. The mechanism is the Private Residential Tenancies Board established by Part 8 of the Act. Section 100(4) of the Housing (Miscellaneous) Provisions Act 2009 removes the requirement of a tenant's signature on the prescribed form for registration under the Act.

Employment Legislation

Action	Time	Section
Working time claim including claim by employee for holidays		
Rights Commissioner or the Employment Appeals Tribunal when ancillary to another claim before the Employment Appeals Tribunal	Six months from date of contravention (can be extended to 18 months if reasonable cause can be shown)	Organisation of Working Time Act 1997, section 27 and section 40
Appeal to Labour Court from decision of Rights Commissioner	Six weeks from date decision is communicated to parties	Organisation of Working Time Act 1997, section 28
Claim in relation to minimum notice		
Employment Appeals Tribunal	No time specified	Minimum Notice and Terms of Employment Act 1973, section 11
Appeal to the High Court on point of law only	No time specified	Minimum Notice and Terms of Employment Act 1973, section 11

(Continued)

Employment Legislation: (*Continued*)

Action	Time	Section
Unfair dismissal claim		
Rights Commissioner or the Employment Appeals Tribunal	Six months from date of dismissal (can be extended to 12 months in exceptional circumstances)	Unfair Dismissals Act 1977, section 8 as amended by section 7(2) of the Unfair Dismissals (Amendment) Act 1993
Appeal to Employment Appeals Tribunal from recommendation of a Rights Commissioner	Within six weeks of the date on which recommendation given to the parties concerned	Unfair Dismissals Act 1977, section 9
Appeal to Circuit Court from determination of the Employment Appeals Tribunal	Within six weeks of the date on which the determination is communicated to the parties	Unfair Dismissals (Amendment) Act 1993, section 11

(Continued)

Employment Legislation: (*Continued*)

Action	Time	Section
Claim for redress in respect of employment-related discrimination or victimisation (including dismissal)		
Director of Equality Tribunal/ Equality Officer or at option of complainant in cases of alleged gender discrimination, the Circuit Court	Six months from the date of the occurrence, or the most recent occurrence, of the act of discrimination or victimisation (can be extended to 12 months for reasonable cause)	Employment Equality Act 1998, section 77 as amended by section 32, Equality Act 2004
Appeal from decision of the Director to the Labour Court	42 days from date of decision	Employment Equality Act 1998, section 83 and section 77(12) as amended by Civil Law (Miscellaneous Provisions) Act 2011

(Continued)

Employment Legislation: (*Continued*)

Action	Time	Section
Appeal from decision of the Director to the High Court on a point of law	21 days or within such further period as the Court, on application made to it by the intending appellant, may allow where the Court is satisfied that there is good and sufficient reason for extending that period and that the extension of the period would not result in an injustice being done to any other person concerned in the matter (Rules of Superior Courts, Order 106/SI 293/2005)	Employment Equality Act 1998, section 79(7) as inserted by section 35, Equality Act 2004

(*Continued*)

Employment Legislation: (*Continued*)

Action	Time	Section
Appeal from the Labour Court to the High Court on a point of law only	21 days on application made to it by the intending appellant, may allow where the Court is satisfied that there is good and sufficient reason for extending that period and that the extension of the period would not result in an injustice being done to any other person concerned in the matter (Rules of Superior Courts, Order 106/SI 293/2005)	Employment Equality Act 1998, section 90 as amended by the Schedule to the Equality Act 2004
Claim for redundancy payments The Employment Appeals Tribunal	52 weeks from the date of dismissal or date of termination of employment or 104 weeks if reasonable cause for failure to claim can be shown to the Employment Appeals Tribunal	Redundancy Payments Act 1967, section 24 as amended by the Redundancy Payments Act 1971, section 12 and section 13 of the 1979 Act

(Continued)

Employment Legislation: (*Continued*)

Action	Time	Section
Payment of wages claim		
Rights Commissioner	Six months beginning on date of contravention (may be extended to 12 months in exceptional circumstances)	Payment of Wages Act 1991, section 6
Appeal to Employment Appeals Tribunal	Six weeks from date on which recommendation is communicated to the parties	Payment of Wages Act 1991, section 7
Terms of employment claim		
Rights Commissioner	Six months beginning on date of termination of employment	Terms of Employment (Information) Act 1994, section 7
Appeal to Employment Appeals Tribunal	Six weeks from date on which recommendation is communicated to the parties	Terms of Employment (Information) Act 1994, section 8

(Continued)

Employment Legislation: (*Continued*)

Action	Time	Section
Claim by a part-time worker Rights Commissioner	Six months from the date of contravention of the Act or date of termination of contract of employment whichever earlier. May be extended by 12 months (18 months total) (if the Rights Commissioner is satisfied that failure to present complaint within period is due to a reasonable cause)	Protection of Employees (Part-Time Work) Act 2001, section 16
Appeal to the Labour Court	Six weeks from the date on which the decision to which it relates was communicated to the party	Protection of Employee (Part-Time Work) Act 2001, section 17
Appeal to the High Court on a point of law	21 days (Rules of Superior Courts, Order 84C Rule 2)	Protection of Employees (Part-Time Work) Act 2001, section 17

(*Continued*)

Employment Legislation: (*Continued*)

Action	Time	Section
Claim by a fixed-term worker		
Rights Commissioner	Six months from the date of contravention of the Act or date of termination of contract of employment, whichever earlier. May be extended by 12 months (18 months total) (if the Rights Commissioner is satisfied that failure to present complaint within period is due to a reasonable cause)	Protection of Employees (Fixed-Term Work) Act 2003, section 14
Appeal to the Labour Court	Six weeks from the date on which the decision to which it relates was communicated to the party	Protection of Employee (Fixed-Term Work) Act 2003, section 15
Appeal to the High Court on a point of law	21 days (Rules of Superior Courts, Order 84C Rule 2)	Protection of Employees (Fixed-Term Work) Act 2003, section 15

(Continued)

Employment Legislation: (*Continued*)

Action	Time	Section
Maternity protection claim Rights Commissioner	Six months from date employer informed that employee is pregnant, has given birth, is breastfeeding or if employee is father of child, the expectant mother of the child is pregnant or that child's mother has died (may be extended to 12 months in exceptional circumstances)	Maternity Protection Act 1994, section 31 as amended by the Maternity Protection (Amendment) Act 2004, section 21
Appeal to Employment Appeals Tribunal	Four weeks from date on which decision is communicated to the parties	Maternity Protection Act 1994, section 33

(*Continued*)

Employment Legislation: (*Continued*)

Action	Time	Section
Adoptive leave claim Rights Commissioner	Six months from the day of placement or, where no placement, six months from date employer first notified of parent's intention to take leave or, in the case of an adoptive father, six months from the death of adoptive mother (may be extended to 12 months in exceptional circumstances)	Adoptive Leave Act 1995, section 34
Appeal to Employment Appeals Tribunal	Four weeks from date on which decision is communicated to the parties	Adoptive Leave Act 1995, section 35
Young persons' employment claim Rights Commissioner	Six months beginning on date of contravention of sections 13 or 17 (may be extended to 12 months in exceptional circumstances)	Protection of Young Persons (Employment) Act 1996, section 18(4)

(*Continued*)

Employment Legislation: (*Continued*)

Action	Time	Section
Appeal to Employment Appeals Tribunal	Six weeks from date on which recommendation is communicated to the parties	Protection of Young Persons (Employment) Act 1996, section 19
Parental leave claim Rights Commissioner	Six months after occurrence of dispute relating to entitlements	Parental Leave Act 1998, section 18
Appeal to Employment Appeals Tribunal	Within four weeks of date on which decision is communicated to the parties	Parental Leave Act 1998, section 19
Minimum wage claim Rights Commissioner	Six months after statement obtained or time elapsed for its production under section 23 (may be extended to 12 months)	National Minimum Wage Act 2000, section 24
Appeal to Labour Court	Within six weeks of date on which decision is communicated to the parties	National Minimum Wage Act 2000, section 27

(Continued)

Employment Legislation: (*Continued*)

Action	Time	Section
Carer's leave claim Rights Commissioner	Within six months of date of contravention giving rise to dispute (may be extended to 12 months if reasonable to do so)	Carer's Leave Act 2001, sections 19(3) and (8)
Appeal to Employment Appeals Tribunal	Within four weeks of date on which decision is communicated to the parties	Carer's Leave Act 2001, section 20(2)
Trade disputes Objection to an investigation of the dispute by a Rights Commissioner	Three weeks after the notice has been sent by post to the party	Industrial Relations Act 1990, section 36
Appeal to the Labour Court against the recommendations of a Rights Commissioner	Six weeks from the date of the recommendation by the Rights Commissioner	Industrial Relations Act 1990, section 36
Application to the Circuit Court to enforce determination of Labour Court	Where period specified in the determination has expired or, if no such period specified, as soon as may be after the determination is communicated to the parties	Industrial Relations Act 2001, section 10 as amended by Industrial Relations (Miscellaneous Provisions) Act 2004, section 4

(Continued)

123

Employment Legislation: (*Continued*)

Action	Time	Section
Complaint to Rights Commissioner for alleged victimisation arising out of trade dispute	Within six months of the occurrence of the alleged victimisation (may be extended to 12 months if reasonable to do so)	Industrial Relations Act 2004, section 9
Appeal to Labour Court	Six weeks from the date of the decision of the Rights Commissioner or such greater period as the Labour Court may determine in the particular circumstances	Industrial Relations Act 2004, section 10
Claim for redress in respect of discrimination in connection with the provision of goods, services, property and other services to the public		
Director of Equality Tribunal/ Equality Officer	Complaint must be notified to respondent within 2 months from date of prohibited conduct (may be extended to 4 months for reasonable cause or, exceptionally, may be waived)	Equal Status Act 2000, sections 21(2) to 21(4) (as amended by section 54 of the Equality Act 2004) and Intoxicating Liquor Act 2003, section 19

(Continued)

Employment Legislation: (Continued)

Action	Time	Section
The Director's jurisdiction is in all cases except for claims in respect of registered clubs and licensed premises which go before the District Court	Complaint must be lodged with Tribunal within 6 months from date of the prohibited conduct or from date of the most recent occurrence (may be extended to 12 months for reasonable cause)	Equal Status Act 2000, sections 21(6) and (7) (as amended by section 54, Equality Act 2004)
Appeal to the Circuit Court from decision of the Director	42 days from date of decision	Equal Status Act 2000, section 28
Appeal to the Circuit Court from decision of the Director with regard to an extension of time under sections 21(3) and 21(7), Equal Status Act 2000 as amended	42 days from date of decision	Equal Status Act 2000, section 21(7A)(a) as inserted by section 54 of the Equality Act 2004 and amended by Civil Law (Miscellaneous Provisions) Act 2011
Appeal to the High Court from Circuit Court on a point of law only	Rules of Superior Courts	Equal Status Act 2000, section 28(3) and section 21(7A)(c) as inserted by section 54 of the Equality Act 2004 as amended by Civil Law (Miscellaneous Provisions) Act 2011

Reproduced from the Law Directory 2012 with the kind permission of the Law Society of Ireland.

125

Appendix IV

Legal Services Bill – Complaints and Disciplinary Hearings

Complaints and Disciplinary Hearings in Respect of Legal Practitioners
Chapter 1
Complaints

Misconduct by legal practitioners.

45.—(1) An act or omission of a legal practitioner may be considered as constituting misconduct where—

(*a*) the act or omission involves fraud or dishonesty,

(*b*) the act or omission is connected with the provision of legal services, where the legal practitioner has fallen short, to a substantial degree, of the standards reasonably expected of a legal practitioner,

(*c*) the act or omission, where occurring otherwise than in connection with the practice of law, would justify a finding that the legal practitioner concerned is not a fit and proper person to engage in legal practice,

(*d*) the act or omission consists of an offence under this Act or, in the case of a solicitor, an offence under the Solicitors Acts 1954 to 2011,

(e) the act or omission, in the case of a legal practitioner who is a barrister, is likely to bring the barristers' profession into disrepute,

(f) the act or omission, in the case of a legal practitioner who is a solicitor, is likely to bring the solicitors' profession into disrepute,

(g) the act or omission consists of the commission of an arrestable offence,

(h) the act or omission consists of the commission of a crime or offence outside the State which, if committed within the State, would be an arrestable offence,

(i) the act consists of issuing a bill of costs which is excessive.

(2) In this section "arrestable offence" has the same meaning as it has in the Criminal Law Act 1997.

Investigation of complaints in respect of legal practitioners.

46.—(1) Subject to the provisions of this Part, on the coming into operation of this Part, a person who wishes to make a complaint that a legal practitioner has, by act or omission, been guilty of misconduct shall make the complaint to the Authority.

(2) *Subsection (1)* shall not act to prevent the Authority or a person who is aggrieved by the act or omission of a legal practitioner seeking assistance from a person with a view to resolving the issue to which a complaint relates.

Investigation on own initiative.

47.—The Authority may initiate an investigation into the practice of a legal practitioner at any time for the purpose of establishing whether or not the legal practitioner concerned is in compliance with—

(a) the provisions of this Act,

(b) regulations made under this Act, and

(c) in the case of a solicitor—
(i) the provisions of the Solicitors Acts 1954 to 2011,
(ii) regulations made under the Solicitors Acts 1954 to 2011.

Admissibility of complaints.
48.—(1) A complaint shall not be considered by the Authority if in the opinion of the Authority—
(a) it is frivolous or vexatious, or
(b) it is without substance or foundation.
(2) The Authority shall not consider a complaint in respect of a solicitor where it is satisfied that the act or omission to which the complaint relates is—
(a) the same or substantially the same act or omission as that which was the subject matter of a complaint in respect of that solicitor which was previously determined under the Solicitors Acts 1954 to 2011—
(i) by the High Court,
(ii) by the Solicitors Disciplinary Tribunal,
(iii) by the Solicitors Disciplinary Committee, or
(iv) by the Law Society,
or
(b) the same or substantially the same act or omission as that which was the subject of civil proceedings or criminal proceedings in respect of which a final determination of the issues has been made by the court in those proceedings in favour of the solicitor concerned.
(3) The Authority shall not consider a complaint in respect of a barrister where it is satisfied that the act or omission to which the complaint relates is—
(a) the same or substantially the same act or omission as that which was the subject matter of a complaint in respect of that barrister which was previously determined by the Barristers Professional Conduct Tribunal, or

(*b*) the same or substantially the same act or omission as that which was the subject of civil proceedings or criminal proceedings in respect of which a final determination of the issues has been made by the court in those proceedings in favour of the barrister concerned.

(4) The Authority may make Regulations (consistent with this Act) regarding—

(*a*) the making of complaints to the Authority under this Act, and

(*b*) the procedures to be followed by the Authority and the Complaints Committee in investigating complaints under this Act.

(5)(*a*) Where the Authority is satisfied that the complaint is likely to be resolved by mediation or other informal means (including through the intervention of the body which, in relation to the legal practitioner concerned, is the relevant professional body) between the complainant and the legal practitioner concerned, it may invite those parties to attempt to resolve the issue the subject of the complaint in that manner and where it so invites the parties to attempt to resolve the issue it shall not take any further action in relation to the complaint until the parties have done so.

(*b*) Where the Authority has invited the complainant and the legal practitioner to resolve the issue the subject of the complaint and—

(i) a reasonable period of time has passed without the issue having been resolved, or

(ii) the Authority is satisfied that the complaint is unlikely to be resolved by mediation or other informal means,

the Authority shall notify in writing the parties concerned to that effect and proceed to investigate the complaint in accordance with this Part.

130

Complaints Committee authorised to perform functions of Authority under this Part.

49.—The functions of the Authority under this Part shall be performed by a committee to be known as the Complaints Committee, where so authorised either generally or by reference to a specific matter and which is appointed pursuant to section 50.

Membership of Complaints Committee.

50.—(1) The Complaints Committee shall be appointed by the Authority with the approval of the Minister and shall consist of not more than 16 members of whom—

(*a*) the majority shall be lay persons,

(*b*) not less than 3 shall be persons nominated by the Law Society, each of whom has practised in the State as a solicitor for more than 10 years, and

(*c*) not less than 3 shall be persons nominated by the Bar Council, each of whom has practised in the State as a barrister for more than 10 years.

(2) In appointing lay persons to be members of the Complaints Committee, the Authority shall ensure that among those members there are persons who have knowledge of, and expertise in relation to, one or more of the following:

(*a*) the provision of legal services;

(*b*) the maintenance of standards in professions regulated by a statutory body;

(*c*) dealing with complaints;

(*d*) commercial matters;

(*e*) the needs of consumers of legal services.

(3) A person who is not a member of the Authority may be appointed to be a member of the Complaints Committee.

(4) The Complaints Committee shall act in divisions of not less than 3 members and each division (in this Act

referred to as a "Divisional Committee") shall consist of a majority of lay persons.

(5) A Divisional Committee shall consist of an uneven number of members.

(6) Subject to *subsections (4)* and *(5)*, where a complaint relates to a solicitor the Divisional Committee shall include at least one solicitor.

(7) Subject to *subsections (4)* and *(5)*, where a complaint relates to a barrister the Divisional Committee shall include at least one barrister.

Investigation of complaints.

51.—(1) A Divisional Committee shall, having determined that the complaint is an admissible complaint and, in a case where the Divisional Committee has invited the complainant and the legal practitioner to resolve the issue the subject of the complaint, the complaint has not been resolved in that manner, give notice to the legal practitioner of the nature of the complaint and invite the legal practitioner to furnish the Divisional Committee with his or her explanation of the matter within a period specified in the notice.

(2) Where the Divisional Committee receives an explanation which indicates that the act or omission did not constitute misconduct it shall furnish a copy of the explanation to the complainant inviting him or her to furnish observations to the Divisional Committee in relation to the explanation of the legal practitioner within such a period as may be specified by the Divisional Committee.

(3) Where—

(a) the response of the legal practitioner does not satisfy the Divisional Committee that the act or omission did not constitute misconduct, or

(b) the legal practitioner does not furnish a response within the period specified in the notice, the Divisional Committee shall determine whether or not the act or omission the subject of the complaint appears to constitute misconduct.

(4) Where the Divisional Committee determines that the act or omission does not constitute misconduct it shall so advise the complainant and the legal practitioner, giving reasons for the determination.

(5) Where the Divisional Committee determines that the act or omission the subject of the complaint appears to constitute misconduct and that such conduct is of a kind that it considers one or more of the measures specified in *subsection (6)* to be the appropriate manner of determining the complaint it may, where the complainant and the legal practitioner consent in writing, so direct the legal practitioner to act accordingly and where the legal practitioner acts as so directed the complaint shall be considered as determined.

(6) The measures referred to in *subsection (5)* are the following:

(*a*) a direction to the legal practitioner to perform or complete the legal service the subject of the complaint or a direction to the legal practitioner to arrange for the performance or completion of the legal service the subject of the complaint by a legal practitioner nominated by the complainant at the expense of the legal practitioner the subject of the complaint;

(*b*) the issue of a caution to the legal practitioner in respect of the act or omission the subject of the complaint;

(*c*) a direction to the legal practitioner that he or she participate in one or more modules of a professional competence scheme and that he or she furnish evidence to the Authority of such participation within a specified period;

(*d*) a direction to the legal practitioner—

(i) that he or she waive all or a part of any fees otherwise payable by the complainant to the legal practitioner concerned, or

(ii) that he or she refund to the client some or all of any fees paid to the legal practitioner concerned in respect of the legal services the subject of the complaint.

(7) Where—

(a) it appears to the Divisional Committee that the act or omission the subject of the complaint constitutes misconduct and that such misconduct is not of a kind that could properly be dealt with under *subsections (5)* and *(6)*, or

(b) either the complainant or the legal practitioner does not consent to the complaint being disposed of under *subsections (5)* and *(6)*,

the Divisional Committee shall—

(i) recommend to the Authority that it bring an application in respect of the matter to the Legal Practitioners Disciplinary Tribunal for the holding of an inquiry as to whether or not the act or omission complained of constitutes misconduct, or

(ii) if the Divisional Committee considers that the complaint requires further consideration it may investigate the matter further which investigation may include requesting an inspector appointed under *section 27* to attend at the practice of the legal practitioner and exercise any of the powers exercisable by such an inspector pursuant to *section 28*.

(8) Following such further investigation pursuant to *subsection (7)(ii)*, the Divisional Committee shall further consider the matter in accordance with this section.

(9) Where pursuant to *subsection (7)(i)* the Divisional Committee recommends to the Authority that it bring an application to the Legal Procedures Disciplinary Tribunal

for the holding of an inquiry, the Authority shall accept the recommendation.

Chapter 2
Legal Practitioners Disciplinary Tribunal

Establishment of Legal Practitioners Disciplinary Tribunal.
52.—There shall stand established a body to be known as the Legal Practitioners Disciplinary Tribunal to consider applications brought before it by the Authority under section 54 as to whether a specified act or omission by a legal practitioner constitutes misconduct and to perform the other functions assigned to it by this Act.

Membership of Disciplinary Tribunal.
53.—(1) The Disciplinary Tribunal shall be appointed by the Government on the nomination of the Minister and shall consist of not more than 16 members of whom—

(*a*) the majority shall be lay persons,

(*b*) not less than 3 shall be persons, nominated by the Law Society, each of whom has practised in the State as a solicitor for more than 10 years, and

(*c*) not less than 3 shall be persons, nominated by the Bar Council, each of whom has practised in the State as a barrister for more than 10 years.

(2) In nominating lay persons for appointment by the Government as members of the Disciplinary Tribunal, the Minister shall ensure that among those persons nominated there are persons who have knowledge of, and expertise in relation to, one or more of the following:

(*a*) the provision of legal services;

(*b*) the maintenance of standards in professions regulated by a statutory body;

(*c*) the handling of complaints;

(*d*) commercial matters;

(*e*) the needs of consumers of legal services.

(3) The Disciplinary Tribunal shall act in divisions of not less than 3 members and each division shall consist of a majority of lay persons.

(4) There shall be an uneven number of members in each division of the Disciplinary Tribunal.

(5) Subject to *subsections (3)* and *(4)* where a complaint relates to a solicitor the division of the Disciplinary Tribunal shall include at least one solicitor.

(6) Subject to *subsections (3)* and *(4)* where a complaint relates to a barrister the division of the Disciplinary Tribunal shall include at least one barrister.

Applications to Disciplinary Tribunal.

54.—An application for the holding of an inquiry may be brought before the Disciplinary Tribunal by the Authority—

(*a*) where the Complaints Committee has determined that an act or omission of a legal practitioner the subject of a complaint appears to constitute misconduct and that such misconduct is not of a kind that could properly be dealt with by the Authority under *subsection (5)* of *section 51*, or the complainant or the legal practitioner does not consent to the matter being disposed of by the Authority under those provisions, or

(*b*) where the Complaints Committee has, following an investigation undertaken by it under *section 51*, formed the view that an act or omission of a legal practitioner appears to constitute misconduct.

Presentation of case to Disciplinary Tribunal.

55.—The Authority, or a person appointed to do so on its behalf, shall present the evidence to the Disciplinary

Tribunal grounding the contention that misconduct by the legal practitioner concerned has occurred.

Regulations relating to Disciplinary Tribunal.

56.—(1) The Disciplinary Tribunal may make Regulations, consistent with this Act, regulating—

(a) the making of applications to the Disciplinary Tribunal under this Act,

(b) the proceedings of the Disciplinary Tribunal under this Act.

(2) Regulations made under *subsection (1)* may make provision for—

(a) the procedures to be followed in relation to the matters referred to in *subsection (1)*, and

(b) the parties, other than the Authority, the complainant and the legal practitioner concerned, who may make submissions to the Disciplinary Tribunal.

(3) The Disciplinary Tribunal in making Regulations under *subsection (1)*, shall have as objectives that the manner of making applications, and the conduct of proceedings, be as informal as is consistent with the principles of fair procedures, and that undue expense is not likely to be incurred by any party who has an interest in the application.

(4) The Disciplinary Tribunal may consider and determine an application to it under this Chapter on the basis of affidavits and supporting documentation and records where the legal practitioner, the complainant and the Authority consent.

Powers of Disciplinary Tribunal as to taking of evidence, etc.

57.—(1) The Disciplinary Tribunal shall, for the purposes of any inquiry under this Chapter, have the powers, rights and privileges vested in the High Court or a judge thereof on the hearing of an action, in respect of—

(a) the enforcement of the attendance of witnesses and their examination on oath or otherwise,

(b) the compelling of the production of documents, and

(c) the compelling of the discovery under oath of documents,

and a summons signed by a member of the Disciplinary Tribunal may be substituted for and shall be equivalent to any formal procedure capable of being issued in an action for enforcing the attendance of witnesses and compelling the production and the discovery under oath of documents.

(2) The Disciplinary Tribunal may require the Authority and the respondent legal practitioner to submit in writing an outline of the evidence expected to be given by each of the witnesses whom they propose to have summoned to attend the hearing.

(3) The Disciplinary Tribunal may, if of opinion that the evidence expected to be given by any witness whom it is proposed to have summoned to attend the hearing is irrelevant or does not add materially to that proposed to be given by other witnesses and that accordingly the attendance of the witness at the inquiry is likely to give rise to unnecessary delay or expense, may so inform the Authority or respondent legal practitioner, as the case may be, and bring to the attention of the Authority or respondent legal practitioner, the provisions of *subsection (4)*.

(4) On the completion of the inquiry the Disciplinary Tribunal, whether or not it has acted in accordance with *subsection (3)*, may, if of opinion that the attendance of any witness summoned at the request of the complainant or respondent legal practitioner was unnecessary

and thereby involved the witness in avoidable expense, by order direct that the Authority or respondent legal practitioner, as the case may be, shall pay a specified amount or amounts not exceeding €1,000 to the witness in respect of the expense incurred, and the witness may recover the sum or sums from the Authority or respondent legal practitioner, as the case may be, as a simple contract debt.

(5) Before making an order under *subsection (4)*, the Disciplinary Tribunal shall notify in writing the complainant or respondent legal practitioner that it proposes to do so and shall consider any representations that may be made to it in writing by the person concerned within 14 days after the notification.

(6) The Authority or respondent legal practitioner in respect of whom an order has been made under *subsection (4)* may appeal to the High Court against the order within 21 days of the receipt by him or her of notification referred to in *subsection (4)*, and the Court may make such order on the appeal as it thinks fit.

(7) If a person—

(*a*) on being duly summoned as a witness before the Disciplinary Tribunal, without just cause or excuse disobeys the summons,

(*b*) being in attendance as a witness before the Disciplinary Tribunal, refuses to take an oath when required by the Disciplinary Tribunal to do so, or to produce or discover under oath any documents in his or her possession or under his or her control or within his or her procurement legally required by the Disciplinary Tribunal to be produced or discovered under oath by him or her, or to answer any question to which the Disciplinary Tribunal may legally require an answer,

(c) wilfully gives evidence to the Disciplinary Tribunal which is material to its inquiry which he or she knows to be false or does not believe to be true,

(d) by act or omission, obstructs or hinders the Disciplinary Tribunal in the performance of its functions, or

(e) fails, neglects or refuses to comply with the provisions of an order made by the Disciplinary Tribunal, the person shall be guilty of an offence.

(8) A witness before the Disciplinary Tribunal shall be entitled to the same immunities and privileges as if he or she were a witness before the High Court.

(9) A person guilty of an offence under this section shall be liable—

(a) on summary conviction, to a class B fine or to imprisonment for a term not exceeding 6 months or to both, or

(b) on conviction on indictment, to a fine not exceeding €30,000 or to imprisonment for a term not exceeding 2 years or to both.

(10) Section 13 of the Criminal Procedure Act 1967 shall apply in relation to an offence under this section as if, in lieu of the penalties specified in *subsection (3)* of that section, there were specified therein the penalties provided for by *subsection (9)*, and the reference in *subsection (2)(a)* of that section to the penalties provided for in *subsection (3)* of that section shall be construed accordingly.

Inquiry by Disciplinary Tribunal.

58.—(1) Where the Disciplinary Tribunal receives an application from the Authority for the holding of an inquiry, it shall arrange a date for the hearing and notify in writing the respondent legal practitioner, the complainant and the Authority.

(2) Unless the Disciplinary Tribunal considers that it is not necessary to do so, and the legal practitioner, the complainant and the Authority consent, the inquiry shall be conducted by way of oral hearing.

(3) Where an inquiry is held otherwise than by way of oral hearing the Disciplinary Tribunal shall conduct the inquiry by considering affidavits and supporting documentation and records furnished to it.

(4) Unless *subsections (2)* and *(3)* apply, a person appointed by the Authority to do so on its behalf, shall present the case to the Disciplinary Tribunal grounding the contention that misconduct by the respondent legal practitioner concerned has occurred.

(5) The hearing of an inquiry by the Disciplinary Tribunal shall be held otherwise than in public.

(6) The respondent legal practitioner, the complainant and the Authority may be represented at any hearing before the Disciplinary Tribunal by a legal practitioner.

(7) Witnesses appearing before the Disciplinary Tribunal shall give evidence on oath.

(8) The respondent legal practitioner and the complainant shall have an opportunity to examine every witness giving evidence to the Disciplinary Tribunal.

(9) Having conducted the inquiry, the Disciplinary Tribunal shall make a determination whether or not, on the basis of the evidence properly before it, the act or omission to which the inquiry relates constitutes misconduct and, in that event, make a determination as to whether the issue of sanction should be dealt with pursuant to *section 59* or *60*.

Sanctions following finding of misconduct by Disciplinary Tribunal.

59.—Where, pursuant to the holding of an inquiry under this Chapter, the Disciplinary Tribunal makes a finding that there has been misconduct on the part of a legal practitioner and determines that the issue of sanction should be dealt with pursuant to this section, the Disciplinary Tribunal may make an order imposing one or more of the following sanctions on the legal practitioner:

(a) a reprimand;

(b) a warning;

(c) a caution;

(d) a direction that the legal practitioner participate in one or more modules of a professional competence scheme and to furnish evidence to the Disciplinary Tribunal of such participation within a specified period;

(e) a direction that the legal practitioner concerned—

(i) waive all or a part of any costs otherwise payable by the complainant to the legal practitioner concerned in respect of the matter the subject of the complaint,

(ii) refund all or any part of any costs paid to the legal practitioner concerned in respect of the matter the subject of the complaint;

(f) a direction that the legal practitioner arrange for the completion of the legal service to which the inquiry relates or the rectification, at his or her own expense, of any error, omission or other deficiency arising in connection with the provision of the legal services the subject of the inquiry, as the Disciplinary Tribunal may specify;

(g) a direction that the legal practitioner take, at his or her own expense, such other action in the interests of the client as the Disciplinary Tribunal may specify;

(h) a direction that the legal practitioner transfer any documents relating to the subject matter of the complaint (but not otherwise) to another legal practitioner nominated by the client or by the Authority with the consent of the client, subject to such terms and conditions as the Authority may deem appropriate having regard to the circumstances, including the existence of any right to possession or retention of such documents or any of them vested in the legal practitioner or in any other person; and

(*i*) a direction that the whole or a part of the costs of the Disciplinary Tribunal or of any person making submissions to it or appearing before it, in respect of the inquiry be paid by the respondent legal practitioner (which costs shall be assessed by the Legal Costs Adjudicator in default of agreement).

Further provisions regarding sanctions following finding of misconduct by Disciplinary Tribunal.

60.—(1) Where, pursuant to the holding of an inquiry under this Chapter, the Disciplinary Tribunal makes a finding that there has been misconduct by a legal practitioner and determines that the issue of sanction should be dealt with pursuant to this section, the Disciplinary Tribunal shall make a recommendation to the High Court:

(*a*) that the legal practitioner be censured and that he or she pay an amount of money to the Authority or the complainant, as the Court considers appropriate;

(*b*) that the legal practitioner be restricted as to the type of work which he or she may engage in, for such period as the Court considers appropriate and subject to such terms and conditions as the Court considers appropriate;

(*c*) that the legal practitioner be prohibited from practising as a legal practitioner otherwise than as an employee, and subject to such terms and conditions as the Court considers appropriate;

(*d*) that the legal practitioner be suspended from practice as a legal practitioner for a specified period and subject to such terms and conditions as the Court considers appropriate;

(*e*) in the case of a barrister, that the name of the barrister be struck off the roll of practising barristers;

(*f*) in the case of a solicitor, that the name of the solicitor be struck off the roll of solicitors;

(*g*) in the case of a legal practitioner to whom a Patent has been granted, that the Authority make an application referred to in *section 114(2)* in respect of that grant.

(2) In this section and *section 63*, "Patent" has the same meaning as it has in Part II, and includes a Patent granted in the State before the coming into operation of this section.

Persons who may appeal determination of Disciplinary Tribunal and matters in respect of which appeal may be brought.

61.—(1) Where the Disciplinary Tribunal makes a determination that the act or omission concerned does not constitute misconduct, the complainant or the Authority may appeal that finding to the High Court.

(2) Where the Disciplinary Tribunal makes a determination that the act or omission concerned constitutes misconduct and deals with the issue of sanction under section 59 an appeal may be brought to the High Court—

(*a*) by the respondent legal practitioner as respects the determination of misconduct or the sanction imposed,

(*b*) by the complainant as respects the sanction imposed, and

(*c*) by the Authority as respects the sanction imposed.

(3) Where the Disciplinary Tribunal makes a determination that the act or omission concerned constitutes misconduct and deals with the matter under *section 60*, the respondent legal practitioner may appeal that determination to the High Court.

(4) Where the respondent legal practitioner does not appeal the determination of the Disciplinary Tribunal in accordance with *subsection (3)* the High Court shall proceed to deal with the matter in accordance with *section 63*.

Appeals to High Court from Disciplinary Tribunal.
62.—(1) Where a person who by virtue of *section 61* may bring an appeal to the High Court brings such an appeal within the period of 28 days of the date on which the determination in writing was sent to the parties concerned by the Disciplinary Tribunal, the High Court shall determine with the appeal in accordance with this section and any rules of court made in relation to such appeals.

(2) Each party who was a party participating in the inquiry of the Disciplinary Tribunal shall be entitled to appear and make submissions in connection with the matter under appeal.

(3) Where the appeal is brought by a complainant as respects a determination by the Disciplinary Tribunal that the act or omission concerned did not constitute misconduct, the High Court may—

    (*a*) confirm the determination of the Disciplinary Tribunal, or

    (*b*) allow the appeal, and impose a sanction which the Disciplinary Tribunal could impose pursuant to *section 59* or impose a sanction which the Disciplinary Tribunal could have recommended to the High Court pursuant to *section 60*.

(4) Where the Disciplinary Tribunal deals with the matter under *section 60* and the appeal is brought—

    (*a*) by the respondent legal practitioner as respects the determination of misconduct or the sanction imposed,

    (*b*) by the complainant as to the sanction imposed, or

    (*c*) by the Authority as to the sanction imposed,

the High Court may make an order—

(i) confirming that the act or omission the subject of the inquiry does constitute misconduct,

(ii) determining that the act or omission the subject of the inquiry does not constitute misconduct,

(iii) confirming that the sanction imposed by the Disciplinary Tribunal was appropriate,

(iv) determining that the sanction imposed by the Disciplinary Tribunal was not the appropriate sanction and imposing a sanction which the Disciplinary Tribunal could impose pursuant to *section 59* or imposing a sanction which the Disciplinary Tribunal could have recommended to the High Court pursuant to *section 60*.

Consideration of matter by High Court where referred by Disciplinary Tribunal.

63.—(1) Where a matter is referred to the High Court by the Disciplinary Tribunal pursuant to *section 60* and the respondent legal practitioner appeals against the finding of misconduct the Court shall first determine the issue as to whether the act or omission concerned constitutes misconduct.

(2) In respect of that appeal the High Court may—

(*a*) confirm the determination of the Disciplinary Tribunal as to misconduct, or

(*b*) determine that the act or omission concerned did not constitute misconduct.

(3) Where the High Court confirms the determination of the Disciplinary Tribunal it shall, having given each party who was a party participating in the inquiry of the Disciplinary Tribunal an opportunity to appear to make submissions in connection with the matter—

(*a*) impose one or more of the sanctions which the Disciplinary Tribunal could impose under *section 59*, or

(*b*) make an order—

(i) that the legal practitioner be censured and that he or she pay an amount of money to the Authority or the complainant, as the Court considers appropriate,

(ii) that the legal practitioner be restricted as to the type of work which he or she may engage in, for such period as the Court considers appropriate and subject to such terms and conditions as the Court considers appropriate,

(iii) that the legal practitioner be prohibited from practising as a legal practitioner otherwise than as an employee, and subject to such terms and conditions as the Court considers appropriate,

(iv) that the legal practitioner be suspended from practice as a legal practitioner for a specified period and subject to such terms and conditions as the Court considers appropriate,

(v) in the case of a barrister, that the name of the barrister be struck off the roll of practising barristers,

(vi) in the case of a solicitor, that the name of the solicitor be struck off the roll of solicitors,

(vii) in the case of a legal practitioner to whom a Patent has been granted, that the Authority make an application referred to in *section 114(2)* in respect of that grant.

Exercise of jurisdiction of High Court under sections 62 and 63.

64.—The jurisdiction vested in the High Court by *sections 62* and *63* shall be exercised by the President of the High Court or, if and whenever the President of the High Court so directs, by an ordinary judge of the High Court for the time being assigned in that behalf by the President of the High Court.

Appeals to Supreme Court.

65.—The Authority or the legal practitioner concerned may appeal to the Supreme Court against an order of the High Court made under *section 63* within a period of 21 days beginning on the date of the order and, unless the High Court or the Supreme Court otherwise orders, the order of the High Court shall have effect pending the determination of such appeal.

Orders made by High Court or determinations made by Authority.

66.—(1) A copy of every order made by the High Court under *section 62* or *63* and any determination made by the Disciplinary Tribunal under *sections 58* to *60* shall be furnished to the registrar of solicitors in the case of an order relating to a solicitor and to the Bar Council in the case of an order relating to a practising barrister.

(2) Where an order—

    (*a*) striking the name of a legal practitioner who is a solicitor off the roll of solicitors,

    (*b*) striking the name of a legal practitioner who is a barrister off the roll of practising barristers, or

    (*c*) suspending a legal practitioner from practice,

is made by the High Court under *section 62* or *63*, the Authority shall as soon as practicable thereafter cause a notice stating the effect of the operative part of the order to be published in *Iris Oifigiúil* and shall also cause the notice to be published in such other manner as the Authority may consider appropriate.

(3) Where a matter is determined by the Disciplinary Tribunal in accordance with *section 59* and the time for

lodging an appeal has expired the Authority shall arrange for the publication of—

(*a*) its determination,

(*b*) the nature of the misconduct,

(*c*) the sanction imposed, and

(*d*) the name of the legal practitioner concerned.

(4) Where the High Court makes an order—

(*a*) under *section 62(3)(b)*,

(*b*) under *section 62(4)* (other than *paragraph (ii)*),

(*c*) under *section 63* (other than *subsection (2)(b)*),

the Authority shall arrange for the publication of—

(i) the finding of misconduct,

(ii) the nature of the misconduct,

(iii) the sanction imposed, and

(iv) the name of the legal practitioner concerned.

Privilege in respect of certain proceedings.

67.—The following shall be absolutely privileged:

(*a*) complaints made to the Authority under this Part and documents created or furnished to the parties entitled to receive them under this Part;

(*b*) proceedings and documents associated with an inquiry held by the Disciplinary Tribunal under this Part;

(*c*) a report made by the Disciplinary Tribunal to the High Court in accordance with this Part;

(*d*) a notice authorised by *section 66* to be published or communicated.

Enforcement of order of Disciplinary Tribunal under this Part.

68.—(1) Where, on application by the Authority in circumstances where the matter is not otherwise before the High Court, it is shown that a legal practitioner or any other person has refused, neglected or otherwise failed, without reasonable cause, to comply in whole or in part with a determination made by the Disciplinary Tribunal under this Part, the Court may by order direct the legal practitioner or other person, as the case may be, to comply in whole or in part as may be appropriate, with the determination of the Disciplinary Tribunal.

(2) An application by the Authority pursuant to *subsection (1)* shall be on notice to the legal practitioner or other person concerned unless the High Court otherwise orders.

(3) An order of the High Court under *subsection (1)* may contain such provisions of a consequential nature as the Court considers appropriate.

Legal Terms Explained

Abstract of Title A list of the documents and facts constituting the vendor's or seller's title to land and certain interests in land prepared when land is sold.

Act of bank-ruptcy A person cannot be made bankrupt merely because they are insolvent, i.e. cannot pay their debts. A petition to make them bankrupt cannot be presented against them until some act of a public nature has taken place in consequence of the financial difficulties of the debtor. These acts are called 'acts of bankruptcy.' The most usual of these acts is failure to comply with a bankruptcy notice, that is, to pay to a creditor who has obtained a judgment from a court the amount due on that judgment when demanded in writing, called a bankruptcy notice.

Act of God Also termed 'viz major', this is an occurrence that has its origin in the agency of natural forces, for example a great and violent storm. Like an inevitable accident, it constitutes a defence to an action for negligence. One such occurrence declared by the High Court in recent years arose out of claims for damage caused by such a storm in Co. Wicklow.

Adjudication order

An order of the court following on the petition and receiving order in bankruptcy that makes a debtor bankrupt, and for the first time takes their property away from them and gives it to a trustee to be divided among their creditors.

Administration action

Any personal representative, i.e. executor or administrator, or beneficiary under a will or intestacy (where no will is made), or any creditor of a deceased person, is entitled to seek the assistance of the court in deciding any question of doubt such as a right to receive a legacy or payment of a debt.

Affidavit

A sworn statement in writing.

Affirmation

This is a substitute for the oath used in cases where the person giving evidence, whether verbally or by affidavit, objects to take the oath because the taking of an oath is contrary to their religious beliefs or they have no religious beliefs. In such a case they are said to 'affirm.' Instead of saying the words of the oath, 'I swear by Almighty God that ...', they say, 'I A.B. do solemnly, sincerely and truly declare and affirm ...'.

Aggravated damages	An increased measure of damages awarded by a court where the defendant's conduct has been so wanton and reckless as to injure the plaintiff to an exceptional degree.
Alternative dispute resolution	Procedures for settling disputes by means other than litigation, e.g. arbitration and mediation.
Appeal	An application to a higher court to revise a decision of an inferior court or tribunal.
Appearance	A document issued by a defendant in a civil action indicating their intention to defend the action.
Arbitration	One of the most common ways in which a right of bringing an action is suspended or stayed is by entering into an agreement to arbitrate upon differences that may arise. Where a person has agreed to arbitration, the courts will not permit them to bring an act on the subject of the dispute until the arbitration has been decided. Arbitration hearings are held in private. Arbitration is generally believed to be less expensive than litigation.
Attorney General	The chief legal adviser to the Government. He/she also represents the public at large when their interests are at stake.
Attorney, power of	A written authority given by one person to another to act legally in their name.

Bailee	A person with whom property is pledged or deposited, e.g. a pawn-broker. The transaction is said to be a 'bailment'; the person to whom the goods belong is called the 'bailor'.
Brief	The written instructions prepared by solicitors for barristers prior to trial.
Certiorari	The writ ordering the removal of a trial from one court to another, e.g. from an inferior to a higher court. If the application is successful, the court may quash the order made by the inferior court or tribunal.
Case stated	A statement of facts prepared by a court in order to get the opinion of a higher court on a point of law.
Caveat	A written notice requesting that nothing be done regarding the estate of a deceased person without notice being given to the person who issued the caveat or their solicitor.
Contempt of court	Conduct offensive to a court or prejudicial to the administration of justice, e.g. publication of an accused person's previous convictions before the jury pronounces its verdict or doing something such as picketing in defiance of a court order.
Copyright	The exclusive right to make copies of an original work.
Counsel	Barristers, including senior counsel and members of the Junior Bar.
Criminal libel	A libel so grave or so dangerous in character that it is the fit subject of criminal proceedings. High Court

approval must be sought before a writ for criminal libel can be issued.

Damages, general
Such damages as the law presumes to have resulted from a civil wrong (a tort) without the plaintiff having to prove special injury.

Damages, special
Direct loss and damage as the plaintiff can prove they suffered as a consequence of the defendant's wrongful conduct.

Damages, exemplary
An amount of damages that is so great or heavy as to make an example of a defendant.

Damages, punitive
An award of heavy damages to punish a defendant in a civil action whose conduct has been of a flagrant nature and a gross infringement of the plaintiff's right. The reason for this is that it is the function of the civil courts to compensate and the function of the criminal courts to punish.

Defamation
The publication of words injurious to another person's character or reputation. There are two kinds, libel and slander.

Discovery
A legal proceeding in the Circuit Court or High Court by which a party to a civil action may voluntarily or by court order disclose under oath any documents in their possession or procurement bearing on the issues in dispute.

Emergency care order
An order placing a child in the care of the Health Service Executive for a

maximum period of eight days if the court is satisfied there is a serious risk to the child's health or welfare.

Ex parte Proceedings conducted on behalf of one party to a civil action in the absence of the other.

In camera A court hearing in which the public is excluded from attending.

Intra vires Within the power of.

Injunction A court order directing a party to do, or to refrain from doing, something. An injunction can be *ad interim* (temporary), interlocutory (continuing) or perpetual (permanent). There are different kinds of injunctions, including a *mareva* injunction, which bars a defendant from removing their assets from the jurisdiction until the trial of an action for a debt due.

Libel A permanent representation, such as writing, the effect of which is to injure a person's good name by holding them to public ridicule, hatred or contempt.

Notary public A solicitor who witnesses the signing of documents or makes copies of them to verify their authenticity.

Mandamus A writ issued by the High Court ordering a lower court to perform some duty.

Mediation A form of alternative dispute resolution that aims to assist two (or more) disputants in reaching an agreement. Whether an agreement results or not, and whatever the content of

	that agreement, if any, the parties themselves determine it rather than accepting something imposed by a third party.
Mortgage suit	A proceeding to recover a debt by forcing a sale of property available to the holder of security on that property.
Plenary summons	The document which commences certain proceedings in the High Court, e.g. damages for personal injuries and libel.
Prima facie	On first view.
Slander	Defamatory words spoken by mouth.
Specific perfor-mance	An order of the court directing a defendant to perform a contract in the plaintiff's favour.
Sub judice	The term used when legal proceedings have been commenced, whether civil or criminal, when public comment is forbidden and breach of it can constitute contempt of court.
Subpoena	A summons addressed to a witness ordering their attendance in court for the hearing of an action.
Ultra vires	Beyond the power of.
Without prejudice	The term used in relation to a letter written or an admission made during negotiations, on the understanding that it will not be used against the party making it in the event of a court action.

Adapted with permission from *Going to Court: A Consumer's Guide* by Damien McHugh (Dublin, First Law: 2002).

Useful Organisations

Information is valid at time of going to print. Please confirm locations and opening hours by phone or website as these details may change.

The Law Society of Ireland
Blackhall Place, Dublin 7
Tel: (01) 672 4800, Monday to Friday, 9:00 a.m. to 5:00 p.m.
Fax: (01) 672 4801
DX: 79 Dublin
Email: general@lawsociety.ie
Website: www.lawsociety.ie

Bar Council
Bar Council Administration Office, Four Courts, Dublin 7
Tel: (01) 817 5000
Fax: (01) 817 5150
Email: barcouncil@lawlibrary.ie
Website: www.lawlibrary.ie

Reception
Four Courts: (01) 872 0622
Distillery Building: (01) 817 4900
Church Street Building: (01) 817 5005

The Courts Service
15–24 Phoenix Street North, Smithfield, Dublin 7
Tel: (01) 888 6000
Website: www.courts.ie

Mediators' Institute of Ireland
35 Fitzwilliam Place, Dublin 2
Tel: (01) 609 9190
Fax: (01) 493 0595
Email: info@themii.ie
Website: www.themii.ie

Dublin International Arbitration Centre
Distillery Building, 145–151 Church Street, Dublin 7
Tel: (01) 817 4663
Fax: (01) 817 4901
Email: info@dublinarbitration.com
Website: www.dublinarbitration.ie

Citizens' Information Service
Citizens Information Board, Ground Floor, George's Quay
House, 43 Townsend Street, Dublin 2
Tel: (076) 107 4000
Website: www.citizensinformation.ie
The Citizens Information Board is a statutory body which
supports the provision of information, advice and advo-
cacy on a broad range of public and social services. A list
of local Citizens Information Centres can be found on its
website.

Money Advice and Budgeting Service
Helpline: (076) 107 2002
Email: helpline@mabs.ie
Website: www.mabs.ie

MABS is a free, confidential, independent and non-judgmental service for people in debt, or in danger of getting into debt, in Ireland. It is a national service with over 60 offices nationwide. A list of local offices can be found on its website.

Consumers' Association of Ireland
43–44 Chelmsford Road, Ranelagh, Dublin 6
Tel: (01) 497 8600
Fax: (01) 497 8601
Email: cai@thecai.ie
Website: www.thecai.ie

Legal Aid Board
Head Office
Quay Street, Cahirciveen, Co. Kerry
Tel: (066) 947 1000
LoCall: 1890 615 200
Fax: (066) 947 1035
Email: info@legalaidboard.ie

Dublin Office
47 Upper Mount Street, Dublin 2
Tel: (01) 644 1900
Fax: (01) 662 3661
Website: www.legalaidboard.ie

List of Law Centres

Cavan Law Centre
Newcourt Shopping Centre, Church Street, Cavan
Tel: (049) 433 1110
Fax: (049) 433 1304
Email: lawcentrecavan@legalaidboard.ie

Clare Law Centre
Unit 6A Merchants Square, Ennis, Co. Clare
Tel: (065) 682 1929
Fax: (065) 682 1939
Email: lawcentreennis@legalaidboard.ie

Pope's Quay Law Centre
Northquay House, Pope's Quay, Cork
Tel: (021) 455 1686
Fax: (021) 455 1690
Email: lawcentrecorknorth@legalaidboard.ie

South Mall Law Centre
1A South Mall, Cork
Tel: (021) 427 5998
Fax: (021) 427 6927
Email: corksouth@legalaidboard.ie

Donegal Law Centre
Unit B9, Letterkenny Town Centre, Justice Walsh Road,
Letterkenny, Co. Donegal
Tel: (074) 912 6177
Fax: (074) 912 6086
Email: lawcentreletterkenny@legalaidboard.ie

Blanchardstown Law Centre
Units 6–8 Blanchardstown Business Centre, Clonsilla
Road, Dublin 15
Tel: (01) 820 0455
Fax: (01) 820 0450
Email: lawcentreblanchardstown@legalaidboard.ie

Clondalkin Law Centre
Tower Shopping Centre, Clondalkin, Dublin 22
Tel: (01) 457 6011

Fax: (01) 457 6007
Email: lawcentreclondalkin@legalaidboard.ie

Dolphin House Office
Third Floor, Dolphin House, East Essex Street, Dublin 2
Tel: (01) 888 6998, (01) 888 6957
Fax: (01) 888 6007
Email: dolphinhousechildcare@legalaidboard.ie

Finglas Law Centre
44–49 Main Street, Finglas, Dublin 11
Tel: (01) 864 0314
Fax: (01) 864 0362
Email: finglaslc@legalaidboard.ie

Gardiner Street Law Centre
45 Lower Gardiner Street, Dublin 1
Tel: (01) 874 5440
Fax: (01) 874 6896
Email: lawcentregardinerstreet@legalaidboard.ie

Brunswick Street Law Centre
48/49 North Brunswick Street/George's Lane, Dublin 7
Tel (01) 646 9600
Fax: (01) 646 9799
Email: brunswickstreet@legalaidboard.ie

Tallaght Law Centre
Village Green, Tallaght, Dublin 24
Tel: (01) 451 1519
Fax: (01) 451 7989
Email: lawcentretallaght@legalaidboard.ie

Galway Law Centre
9 Francis Street, Galway

Tel: (091) 561 650
Fax: (091) 563 825
Email: galwaylawcentre@legalaidboard.ie

Kerry Law Centre
1 Day Place, Tralee, Co. Kerry
Tel: (066) 712 6900
Fax: (066) 712 3631
Email: lawcentretralee@legalaidboard.ie

Kildare Law Centre
Canning Place, Newbridge, Co. Kildare
Tel: (045) 435 777
Fax: (045) 435 766
Email: lawcentrenewbridge@legalaidboard.ie

Kilkenny Law Centre
87 Maudlin Street, Kilkenny
Tel: (056) 776 1611
Fax: (056) 776 1562
Email: lawcentrekilkenny@legalaidboard.ie

Laois Law Centre
Unit 6A Bridge Street, Portlaoise, Co. Laois
Tel: (057) 866 1366
Fax: (057) 866 1362
Email: lawcentreportlaoise@legalaidboard.ie

Limerick Law Centre
Lock Quay, Limerick
Tel: (061) 314 599
Fax: (061) 318 330
Email: lawcentrelimerick@legalaidboard.ie

Longford Law Centre
Credit Union Courtyard, 50A Main Street, Longford
Tel: (043) 334 7590
Fax: (043) 334 7594

Louth Law Centre
Condil House, Roden Place, Dundalk, Co. Louth
Tel: (042) 933 0448
Fax: (042) 933 0991
Email: lawcentredundalk@legalaidboard.ie

Mayo Law Centre
Humbert Mall, Main Street, Castlebar, Co. Mayo
Tel: (094) 902 4334
Fax: (094) 902 3721
Email: lawcentrecastlebar@legalaidboard.ie

Meath Law Centre
Kennedy Road, Navan, Co. Meath
Tel: (046) 907 2515
Fax: (046) 907 2519
Email: lawcentrenavan@legalaidboard.ie

Monaghan Law Centre
Alma House, The Diamond, Monaghan
Tel: (047) 84888
Fax: (047) 84879
Email: monaghanlc@legalaidboard.ie

Offaly Law Centre
Harbour Street, Tullamore, Co. Offaly
Tel: (057) 935 1177
Fax: (057) 935 1544
Email: lawcentretullamore@legalaidboard.ie

Sligo Law Centre
Bridgewater House, Rockwood Parade, Thomas Street, Sligo
Tel: (071) 916 1670
Fax: (071) 916 1681
Email: lawcentresligo@legalaidboard.ie

Tipperary Law Centre
Friars Court, Abbey Street, Nenagh, Co. Tipperary
Tel: (067) 34181
Fax: (067) 34083
Email: lawcentrenenagh@legalaidboard.ie

Waterford Law Centre
Canada House, Canada Street, Waterford
Tel: (051) 855 814
Fax: (051) 871 237
Email: lawcentrewaterford@legalaidboard.ie

Westmeath Law Centre
Payne's Lane, Irishtown, Athlone, Co. Westmeath
Tel: (090) 647 4694
Fax: (090) 647 2160
Email: lawcentreathlone@legalaidboard.ie

Wexford Law Centre
Unit 8 Redmond Square, Wexford
Tel: (053) 912 2622
Fax (053) 912 4927
Email: lawcentrewexford@legalaidboard.ie

Wicklow Law Centre
Bridge Street, Wicklow
Tel: (0404) 66166
Fax: (0404) 66197
Email: lawcentrewicklow@legalaidboard.ie

Part-Time Law Centres

Please note that the dates and times the part-time law centres are open may change depending on demand for the service. Please use the contact numbers below to find out when the law centre is open.

Carlow

Carlow Part-Time Law Centre, St Catherine's Citizens Information Bureau, St Joseph's Road, Carlow
Tel: (059) 913 8700
Open: First and last Friday of every month

Cork

Bantry Part-Time Law Centre, Citizens Information Centre, Bantry, Co. Cork
Tel: (021) 455 1686
Open: Once a month

Donegal

Donegal Part-Time Law Centre, The Courthouse, Donegal Town, Co. Donegal
Tel: (074) 912 6177
Open: Once a month

Kerry

Killarney Part-Time Law Centre, 52 High Street, Killarney, Co. Kerry
Tel: (066) 712 6900
Open: Every Friday morning

Leitrim

Carrick-on-Shannon Part-Time Law Centre, The Health Centre, Leitrim Road, Carrick-on-Shannon, Co. Leitrim
Tel: (043) 47590
Open: Once a month

Louth
Drogheda Part-Time Law Centre, Drogheda Community Services Centre, Scarlet Crescent, Drogheda, Co. Louth
Tel: (041) 983 6084, (041) 983 3490
Open: First and second Tuesday of every month

Mayo
Ballina Part-Time Law Centre, The Pastoral Centre (Cathedral Grounds), Ballina, Co. Mayo
Tel: (094) 902 4334
Open: Once a month

Ballyhaunis Part-Time Law Centre, Health Centre, Knock Road, Ballyhaunis, Co. Mayo
Tel: (094) 902 4334
Open: Fourth Tuesday of every month

Roscommon
Boyle Part-Time Law Centre, Citizens Information Centre, 7 Elphin Street, Boyle, Co. Roscommon
Tel: (071) 916 1670
Open: Once a month

Tipperary
Thurles Part-Time Law Centre, Thurles Community Social Services, Rossa Street, Thurles, Co. Tipperary
Tel: (067) 34181
Open: Second Tuesday of every month

Clonmel Part-Time Law Centre, Citizens Information Centre, 14 Wellington Street, Clonmel, Co. Tipperary
Tel: (052) 22267
Open: Three or four times a month

Westmeath
Mullingar Part-Time Law Centre, Enterprise Centre,
Bishopgate Street, Mullingar, Co. Westmeath
Tel: (090) 647 4694
Open: Once a month

Courtesy of the Legal Aid Board (www.legalaidboard.ie)

FLAC (Free Legal Advice Centres)
13 Lower Dorset Street, Dublin 1
Lo-Call Information and Referral Line: 1890 350 250
Tel: (01) 887 3600
Fax: (01) 874 5320
Website: www.flac.ie

FLAC is an independent human rights organisation
which operates a lo-call telephone information line and,
in conjunction with the Citizens Information Board, a
network of part-time legal advice centres throughout
Ireland. Many FLAC centres are located in local citizens
information centres (CICs). Certain centres specialise
in different areas of law such as family, employment or
immigration. Please check the website or phone ahead if
you wish to visit a specialist centre.

FLAC has a range of downloadable leaflets contain-
ing basic legal information on some legal areas. It also
produces 'FLACsheets' on core campaign areas such as
social welfare, personal debt, consumer credit and civil
legal aid.

Dublin FLAC Centres

Aungier Street
FLAC, Carmelite CIC, Carmelite Community Centre, 56 Aungier Street, Dublin 2
Tel: (076) 107 7110

Balbriggan
FLAC, Balbriggan CIC, Town Hall, St Georges Square, Balbriggan, Co. Dublin
Tel: (076) 107 7450

Ballyboden
FLAC, Whitechurch Library, Taylor's Lane, Ballyboden, Dublin 16
Tel: (01) 495 2020

Ballyfermot
FLAC, Ballyfermot CIC, Community Civic Centre, Ballyfermot Road, Dublin 10
Tel: (076) 107 5000

Ballymun
FLAC, Ballymun CIC, The Library, Ballymun Road, Dublin 9
Tel: (076) 107 7320

Ballymun Civic Centre
FLAC, Ballymun Civic Centre CIC, Main Road, Ballymun, Dublin 9
Tel: (076) 107 7330

Blanchardstown
FLAC, Blanchardstown CIC, Westend House, Block A, Westend Office Park, Snugborough Road, Dublin 15
Tel: (076) 107 5040

Cabra
FLAC, Cabra Resource Centre, Dowth Avenue, Cabra, Dublin 7
Tel: (076) 107 7360

Clondalkin
FLAC, Clondalkin CIC, Oakfield Industrial Estate, 9th Lock Road, Clondalkin, Dublin 22
Tel: (076) 107 5100

Coolock
Northside Community Law Centre, Northside Civic Centre, Bunratty Road, Dublin 17 (Please note that this is not a FLAC Centre.)
Tel: (01) 847 7804

Crumlin
FLAC, Crumlin CIC, 146 Sundrive Road, Crumlin, Dublin 12 (opposite St Bernadette's Church)
Tel: (076) 107 7020

Dundrum
FLAC, Dundrum CIC, Unit 2, Level 5, Dundrum Town Centre, Dublin 14
Tel: (076) 107 7430

Dun Laoghaire
FLAC, Dun Laoghaire CIC, Marina House, Clarence Street, Dun Laoghaire, Co. Dublin
Tel: (076) 107 7400

Finglas
FLAC, Finglas CIC, 1B Finglas Village, Finglas, Dublin 11
Tel: (076) 107 7360

Lucan
FLAC, Lucan CIC, Ballyowen Castle Community Centre, Ballyowen Lane, Lucan, Co. Dublin
Tel: (076) 107 5090

Malahide
FLAC, Malahide CIC, Malahide Library, Main Street, Malahide, Co. Dublin
Tel: (076) 107 7480

Meath Street CIC & SICCDA
FLAC, Liberties CIC & SICCDA, 90 Meath Street, Dublin 8
Tel: (01) 453 6098

North King Street
FLAC, Dublin City North West Citizens Information Service, MACRO Community Resource Centre, 1 Green Street, Dublin 7
Tel: (076) 107 7270

Pearse Street
FLAC, St Andrews Resource Centre, 114–116 Pearse Street, Dublin 2
Tel: (01) 677 1930

Prussia Street
FLAC, Holy Family Parish Centre, 13 Prussia Street, Dublin 7
Tel: (01) 838 3563

Raheny
FLAC, KARE Citizens Community Lane, 5 Sybil Hill Road, Raheny, Dublin 5
Tel: (01) 805 8574

Rathmines
FLAC, Rathmines Community Centre, 7 Wynnefield Road, Rathmines, Dublin 6
Tel: (076) 107 7110

Ringsend
FLAC, Ringsend CIC, Ringsend/Irishtown Community Centre, Thorncastle Street, Dublin 4
Tel: (01) 660 4789

Sean McDermott Street
FLAC, Killarney Court, Buckingham Street Upper (End of Sean McDermott Street Lower), Dublin 1
Tel: (076) 107 7260

Swords
FLAC, Swords CIC, Unit 26 The Plaza, Swords, Co. Dublin
Tel: (076) 107 7510

Tallaght
FLAC, Tallaght CIC, 512 Main Street, Tallaght, Dublin 24
Tel: (076) 107 8340

Countrywide FLAC Centres

Carlow
FLAC, Carlow CIC, St Catherine's Community Services Centre, St Joseph's Road, Carlow
Tel: (076) 107 5130

Cavan
FLAC, Cavan CIC, Townhall Place, Townhall Street, Cavan
Tel: (076) 107 5200

Clare
FLAC, Ennis CIC, Bindon Lane, Bank Place, Ennis, Co. Clare
Tel: (076) 107 5260

FLAC, Kilrush CIC, Francis Street, Kilrush, Co. Clare
Tel: (076) 107 5310

FLAC, Shannon CIC, Unit 1, The Business Centre, Shannon, Co. Clare
Tel: (076) 107 5370

Cork
FLAC, Bantry CIC, Wolfe Tone Square, Bantry, Co. Cork
Tel: (076) 107 8390

FLAC, Blackpool CIC, Blackpool Community Centre, 90 Great William O'Brien Street, Blackpool, Cork
Tel: (076) 107 6890

FLAC, Cork CIC, 80 South Mall, Cork
Tel: (076) 107 6950

FLAC, Mallow CIC, Unit 18.1 Market Square, Mallow, Co. Cork
Tel: (076) 107 8000

Donegal
FLAC, Letterkenny CIC, Public Services Centre, Blaney Road, Letterkenny, Co. Donegal
Tel: (076) 107 5530

Galway
FLAC, Galway CIC, Augustine House, St Augustine Street, Galway
Tel: (076) 107 7600

FLAC, Conradh na Gaeilge, Arus na nGael, 45 Sraid Dominic, Gaillimh
Tel: (091) 567 824

FLAC, Tuam CIC, Dublin Road, Tuam, Co. Galway
Tel: (076) 107 7740

Kerry
FLAC, Listowel CIC, 35 The Square, Listowel, Co. Kerry
Tel: (076) 107 7840

FLAC, Killarney CIC, 78 New Street, Killarney, Co. Kerry
Tel: (076) 107 7820

FLAC, Tralee CIC, 4 Bridge Lane, Tralee, Co. Kerry
Tel: (076) 107 7860

Kildare
FLAC, Athy CIC, 3 Emily Row, Athy, Co. Kildare
Tel: (076) 107 8260

FLAC, Maynooth CIC, Derroon House, Dublin Road, Maynooth, Co. Kildare
Tel: (076) 107 8100

FLAC, Naas CIC, 10 Basin Street, Naas, Co. Kildare
Tel: (076) 107 8280

FLAC, Newbridge CIC, Parish Centre, Station Road, Newbridge, Co. Kildare
Tel: (076) 107 8300

Laois
FLAC, Portlaoise CIC, 27 Main Street, Portlaoise, Co. Laois
Tel: (076) 107 5590

Leitrim
FLAC, Carrick-on-Shannon CIC, Somerview House, Dublin Road, Carrick-on-Shannon, Co. Leitrim
Tel: (076) 107 5670

Limerick
FLAC, Limerick CIC, 54 Catherine Street, Limerick
Tel: (076) 107 5780

Longford
FLAC, Longford CIC, Level One, Longford Shopping Centre, Longford
Tel: (076) 107 5890

Louth
FLAC, Drogheda Community Services, Scarlet Crescent, Drogheda, Co. Louth
Tel: (041) 983 6084

FLAC, Dundalk CIC, 4 Adelphi Court, Long Walk, Dundalk, Co. Louth
Tel: (076) 107 5950

Mayo
FLAC, Ballina CIC, Unit 5a, Cualgarra, Teeling Street, Ballina, Co. Mayo
Tel: (076) 107 5990

FLAC, Castlebar CIC, Cavendish House, Link Road, Castlebar, Co. Mayo
Tel: (076) 107 6040

Meath
FLAC, Ashbourne CIC, Unit 2, Killegland Square, Ashbourne, Co. Meath
Tel: (076) 107 6110

FLAC, Navan CIC, Floor 1, 1 Cannon Row, Navan, Co. Meath
Tel: (076) 107 6150

Monaghan
FLAC, Monaghan CIC, 23 North Road, Monaghan
Tel: (076) 107 6230

Offaly
FLAC, Tullamore CIC, Level One, The Bridge Centre,
Tullamore, Co. Offaly
Tel: (076) 107 6290

Roscommon
FLAC, Boyle CIC, 7 Elphin Street, Boyle, Co. Roscommon
Tel: (076) 107 6330

FLAC, Roscommon CIC, 18 Castle View, Castle Street,
Roscommon
Tel: (076) 107 6380

Sligo
FLAC, Sligo CIC, Units 3 & 4, Bridgewater House,
Rockwood Parade, Sligo
Tel: (076) 107 6390

Tipperary
FLAC, Clonmel CIC, Market Place, Clonmel, Co. Tipperary
Tel: (076) 107 6460

FLAC, Nenagh CIC, 43 Pearse Street, Nenagh, Co.
Tipperary
Tel: (076) 107 6470

FLAC, Thurles CIC, 34/35 Croke Street, Thurles, Co.
Tipperary
Tel: (076) 107 6510

FLAC, Tipperary CIC, Community Centre, St Michael's Street, Tipperary Town, Co. Tipperary
Tel: (076) 107 6540

Waterford
FLAC, Waterford CIC, 37 Lower Yellow Road, Waterford
Tel: (076) 107 6580

FLAC, Dungarvan CIC, Scanlon's Yard, Dungarvan, Co. Waterford
Tel: (076) 107 6550

Westmeath
FLAC, Athlone CIC, St Mary's Square, Athlone, Co. Westmeath
Tel: (076) 107 7610

FLAC, Mullingar CIC, Market House, Market Square, Mullingar, Co. Westmeath
Tel: (076) 107 6660

Wexford
FLAC, Wexford CIC, 28 Henrietta Street, Wexford
Tel: (076) 107 6720

Wicklow
FLAC, Blessington CIC, Blessington Library, Town Centre, Blessington, Co. Wicklow
Tel: (076) 107 6780

FLAC, Bray CIC, 6 The Boulevard, Quinsboro Road, Bray, Co. Wicklow
Tel: (076) 107 6780

FLAC, Arklow CIC, 73 Lower Main Street, Arklow, Co. Wicklow
Tel: (076) 107 6750

FLAC, Wicklow CIC, 9/10 Lower Mall, Wicklow Town, Co. Wicklow
Tel: (076) 107 6840

Courtesy of FLAC (www.flac.ie)

Index

Index

Index